DIVORCE FOR GROWNUPS

2ND EDITION

A Comprehensive Guide
to
Divorce in California

David Magnuson, Esq.

This book is intended to serve as a guide to help you navigate the challenging process of divorce in California. It is not a substitute for personalized advice from a licensed attorney.

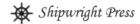 *Shipwright Press*

Copyright © 2010, 2014 by David Magnuson

Manufactured in the United States of America

Library of Congress Cataloging-in-Publication Data
Divorce for grownups : a comprehensive guide to divorce in California /
David Magnuson
p. cm.
Includes index.

1. Divorce – United States – Handbooks, manuals, etc. 2. Communication
in divorce mediation – United States – Handbooks, manuals, etc.

ISBN 978-0-9829353-2-3 Paperback

ISBN 978-0-9829353-1-6 Hardcover

CONTENTS

Introduction: A GRACEFUL DIVORCE?   1

The Financial Cost of Divorce in California   3

Chapter 1: A GUIDE TO HIGH-CONFLICT DIVORCE   5

Chapter 2: MEDIATION   11

How Mediation Works   12

Picking a Mediator   14

Communication During Mediation   19

Mediation v. Litigation – an Illustration   22

Chapter 3: THE DIVORCE PROCESS, STEP BY STEP   39

Chapter 4: DIVISION OF ASSETS AND DEBTS   45

Asset Division, Practically Speaking   46

Putting Together the Financial Puzzle   47

Hiding Assets   53

Dividing the Investment Portfolio   55

The Closely-Held Business   58

Chapter 4: DIVISION OF ASSETS AND DEBTS (cont.)

Stock Options   60

Retirement Benefits   65

Division of Debt   70

Bankruptcy and Divorce   76

The Legal Framework for Asset Division   77

Classification of Property   78

Chapter 5: SPOUSAL SUPPORT   83

Spousal Support, Practically Speaking   84

Sample Cases   86

The Legal Framework for Spousal Support   91

Amount   91

Duration   93

Modifying Spousal Support   95

Taxation and "Alimony Recapture"   96

Family Support   97

Chapter 6: CHILD SUPPORT   107

Child Support, Practically Speaking   102

The Legal Framework for Child Support   102

Chapter 6: CHILD SUPPORT (cont.)

California Formula for Child Support   103

Duration   108

Support Differing from Calculation   109

New Spouse Income and Child Support   111

Other Child-Rearing Expenses   112

Hiding Income   113

Earning Capacity   114

Chapter 7: THE FAMILY HOME   115

The Family Home, Practically Speaking   116

Valuation   117

Capital Gains and Tax Basis   118

Total Housing Costs   121

Calculating Gain   123

The Four Options   129

The Legal Framework of the Family Home   131

Calculating Each Spouse's Share   133

Deferring Sale of the Home   138

Living in the Home Prior to Divorce   139

Chapter 8: CUSTODY   143

Custody, Practically Speaking   145

How You Can Help Your Children   146

Where Will the Children Live?   147

Healthcare   157

Education   158

Holidays   161

Decision Making   162

Dispute Resolution   163

Dealing with Moves   164

Information Exchange   166

Consistency and Ground Rules   168

Hired Help   172

The New Partner   173

The Legal Framework for Custody   176

How Does a Judge Decide on Custody?   176

Is a Child's Choice of Parent Influential?   176

Custody Evaluators – Who Are They?   177

Attorneys for Children   178

Moving Children Away   178

Chapter 9: ESTATE PLANNING AND DIVORCE   181

Estate Planning, Practically Speaking   182

Wills   182

Living Trusts   183

The Legal Framework for Estate Planning   185

Revoking a Living Trust   185

Dividing Irrevocable Trusts   186

Chapter 10: FREQUENTLY ASKED QUESTIONS   187

Appendix: CALIFORNIA FAMILY CODE SECTIONS   199

Custody   199

Child Support   203

Family Support   215

Spousal Support   217

Division of Property   219

DIVORCE FOR GROWNUPS

2ND EDITION

A Comprehensive Guide
to
Divorce in California

INTRODUCTION

The Challenge

"A Graceful Divorce?"

No matter how well each spouse behaves, the process of unwinding a marriage extracts a toll. The process can be alternately sad, terrifying, and infuriating. Even in the most civilized divorce, a certain degree of pain is inevitable.

As a divorce mediator, I strive to make the experience as bearable as possible for my clients. Divorce can be the equivalent of an emotional atom bomb, destroying everything in sight and leaving behind a toxic cloud that lingers for years. The truth is that divorce doesn't have to be so dire. Indeed, many of my clients enjoy the best possible result: a gentle parting of two souls with mutual respect and support for one another. This isn't always achievable, but it happens more frequently than most people suspect.

My personal experience with mediation (I am a divorced father) led me not only to become a mediator myself, but also to write this book. While I am clearly biased in favor of mediation, I hope this book will also provide a valuable source of information for those who follow an alternate path to divorce. Knowledge is power, and a fair settlement can only be obtained when both parties understand their rights under the laws of the State of California and the advantages and disadvantages of different financial and custodial arrangements. This book is intended to provide you with the background you need to come through your divorce intact, both emotionally and financially.

Some readers will find the chapters of this book dealing with divorce mediation valuable, while others will choose to skip directly to the chapters analyzing California family law. I try to strike a balance between high-level advice intended to spare you the misery of a bitterly fought divorce and practical advice examining the mechanics and legal framework surrounding the divorce process. No matter how you use this book, I hope you take one simple axiom to heart:

Act like a grownup.

Doing so will save you a great deal of pain, frustration, and money. No matter how angry your spouse makes you, refrain from the impulse to lash out and drive yourselves further down the litigation highway. Instead, behave respectfully and acknowledge that as awful as this process is for you, acting out of spite will ultimately harm you as much as your spouse. Rather than looking back on your divorce years later with a drained bank account and an overwhelming sense of shame, you will know that you made the best of a tough situation and acted with dignity.

The Financial Cost of Divorce in California

"Failure to Act Reasonably Can Lead to Financial Ruin"

Getting divorced in California can be incredibly expensive. Many divorcing couples watch horror-stricken as everything they have accumulated over a lifetime evaporates in the face of hefty fees charged by attorneys, accountants, appraisers, and other experts. A divorce doesn't have to lead to financial ruin, but it can—easily. To understand how the total fees charged in a divorce can easily run into the tens of thousands of dollars, consider the following scenario, which is not uncommon in a litigated case:

Husband and wife arrive at a settlement conference a few days before trial. The attorneys for each side haven't yet engaged in a serious settlement discussion, and they come to the conference with their expert CPAs in tow. The attorneys each bill at $400 per hour, and the CPAs each bill at $250 per hour. The CPAs get deposed for seven hours. An already astronomical bill reaches stratospheric proportions as the four professionals at the settlement conference bill at a combined rate of over $1300 per hour.

Combined with the cost of discovery (approximately $30,000) and countless previous attorney consultations and memos to file, the cost to settle the case reaches $105,000. (If our fictitious couple can't agree on custody, that figure can easily exceed $200,000.) Needless to say, the financial catastrophe the couple just suffered only compounds the emotional agony of divorce.

Fees in excess of $100,000 may seem outlandish, but it's far too easy to find yourself in a similar situation if you can't negotiate effectively with your spouse. I know of a veterinarian in San Diego whose legal bill at the time of publication of this book was over $600,000. His wife's bill was nearly that amount. Worst of all, settlement was still a distant goal. By the time all is said and done, the combined legal fees for that divorce will exceed $1,500,000. Thankfully this is an extreme example of a divorce gone awry, but it certainly happens.

When I relayed my story about the veterinarian and his wife to an experienced divorce mediator, he chuckled and said that he could have shepherded them through the divorce process for less than $15,000. While it's undoubtedly possible, when one spouse is determined to harm the other, reaching any kind of settlement is challenging at best. It takes a very skilled mediator to make a vindictive spouse see the folly of his or her ways.

At this point you might suspect that I have an agenda: I want all divorces to settle early and fairly, and I am disdainful of long, drawn-out, destructive divorces. To that accusation, I have this response: guilty as charged. I firmly believe that couples have nothing to gain by turning divorce into a battlefield.

CHAPTER 1

A Guide to High-Conflict Divorce

"How to save yourself"

Bombarded with divorce horror stories, the average American might suspect that the spectacularly dramatic unraveling of marriages portrayed in supermarket tabloids and television shows is simply "the way it is." True, divorce is often acrimonious. True, in some cases both spouses act vindictively. And true, divorce is costly, sad, and tremendously stressful.

Yet despite the many challenges that surround divorce, there is hope. *You* can affect the outcome of your own divorce. Yes, your spouse may stoop to sorry levels of human behavior out of fear, anger, or disappointment. Indeed, divorce often triggers the "fight or flight" instinct, a surefire recipe for erratic conduct. But as much as your spouse's behavior infuriates you, you can dramatically increase your chances of achieving a palatable divorce settlement by maintaining your own dignity and refusing to respond when your spouse lashes out. By refraining from joining your spouse in the race to the bottom, you also drastically improve the chance that the two of you will be cordial in the future—a critically important element of any successful co-parenting relationship.

Refusing to debase yourself by acting in conflict with your own standards of conduct may simply sound like window-dressing for the old "turn the other cheek" line. Keep in mind, however, that I'm not suggesting that you play the role of martyr. Divorce is no time to throw your hands up and voluntarily take a beating. Doing so will only ensure that you resent your former spouse for years to come.

Beyond that, doing so might also have catastrophic financial consequences.

To reach a fair settlement and leave the negotiating table with your dignity intact, ask yourself this question before succumbing to the temptation to throw an emotional punch: "In ten years, will I be proud of my conduct?" If you can honestly answer "yes" after navigating the perilous waters of divorce, you will be well poised to move past the experience and embrace a new life unhampered by deep regrets and bitter resentment.

Managing your reaction to your spouse's behavior is one of the greatest challenges of the divorce process. Indeed, keeping a clear head when your heart constricts in disappointment or anger is a difficult task. By following the tips outlined below, though, you may not only save yourself from years of regret, you may also improve your spouse's behavior in the process.

Tip 1: Listen With Care.

As you navigate your way through the exhausting divorce process, you will find yourself distracted by dozens of stressors. The last thing you want to focus on is the stream of words flowing from your spouse's mouth. Indeed, they may even be hurtful. Nevertheless, try to follow the old adage, "Be quick to listen, slow to speak, and slow to become angry." If you are too distracted to listen properly, tell your spouse. And when your spouse is speaking, avoid interrupting. If your spouse really feels that he or she is being *heard*, you can be sure that your negotiations will proceed much more smoothly.

Tip 2: Consider Underlying Feelings.

When your spouse says something truly infuriating, take a deep breath and try to decipher the cause of his or her outburst. Does your spouse feel betrayed, disappointed, or frightened? Step away from the sheer nastiness of his or her comment and search for the underlying wound. You may find that instead of despising your spouse and aching to deliver an equally crippling blow, you feel, frankly, *sorry* for him or her. It may be that there is nothing you can do to steer your spouse towards more productive behavior, but at the very least, understanding the emotional source of his or her actions will help you stay levelheaded.

Tip 3: Refrain from Personal Attacks.

In many cases, a reaction is exactly what an angry spouse wants, and responding to an attack with a counterattack only adds fuel to the fire. No matter how vicious the words that flow from your spouse's mouth, do not respond with equally hateful barbs. This will only escalate the conflict.

Instead of matching your spouse's behavior, try to refocus the conversation. If you want to convey your feelings about a topic, feel free to do so, but avoid using the word, "you." Keep the focus on your own concerns and not the shortcomings of your spouse. For instance, avoid saying, "I know how you are with money, and there is no way I believe that you will use a portion of my child support payments to save for college." Instead, try this, "Having our kids attend college is extremely important to me. If I agree to put a specified sum every month into the children's college savings account, would you consider letting me deduct half that amount from your monthly support payment? That way we will share the responsibility for funding the children's education."

Tip 4: Redirect Tactfully.

If you are using a divorce mediator (which I highly recommend), your mediator should do this for you. However, if you and your spouse are trying to hammer out an agreement on your own, you need to master the art of redirecting the conversation to more productive topics. Your spouse may suddenly want to talk about how you never did your share of household chores. Let your spouse talk first (see Step 1), and then gently tell your spouse that you would like to keep the conversation focused on the topic at hand (child support, for instance).

Tip 5: Don't Let Disagreements Paralyze You.

You and your spouse may not agree on everything. Indeed, you may not agree on much of anything. Regardless, any time you throw a new idea into the mix during divorce settlement negotiations, expect resistance. If your spouse agrees with you, you will be delighted. If he or she doesn't, you will be unfazed. Instead of getting angry when your spouse doesn't see the clear logic of your proposal, you will be better situated to think it through. After a pause (remember, silence is a powerful tool), you can (1) acknowledge your spouse's concern and then offer a better explanation of your proposal, (2) withdraw your proposal (maybe your spouse is right), or (3) offer a compromise.

Tip 6: Focus on Your Common Interests.

You may be thinking, "What common interests?" Well, if you have children with your spouse, the answer is easy. Your children *must* come first, and by focusing on their needs, you and your spouse will be able to move things along. If you don't have children, you probably share a different interest: getting it over with. Nobody enjoys the divorce process, and most couples just want to be done with it. Don't let your eagerness to end the process result in unreasonable concessions, but do remember that you and your spouse both benefit by keeping discussions productive and moving toward the shared goal of putting the divorce behind you.

There is one major exception to the "common interests" theory. When only one spouse has accepted the reality of divorce, a couple may have a very hard road ahead. See Tip #2 above and analyze your spouse's feelings. Could it be that your spouse is sabotaging the process at every turn simply because he or she doesn't want a divorce? If you don't share the common interest of just getting the divorce behind you, intensive mediation and/or therapy might be your best bet.

CHAPTER 2

Mediation

"The path of the grownup"

Divorce litigation has a long and ugly history. It has been the standard way of resolving divorce conflicts for generations, and the cost has always been high. Often emotionally and financially devastating, a litigated divorce ensures that no one wins. Divorcing couples hire lawyers to act as their champions and battle like knights in shining armor, but no one emerges victoriously. Instead of enjoying the satisfaction of a battle well fought, the exhausted parties typically find themselves splitting a vastly diminished prize.

Mediation removes divorce from the adversarial arena. Indeed, the court only plays a minimal role in a mediated divorce. While it's true that divorce always requires a lawsuit (and therefore a certain degree of paperwork), in nearly every case a judge will happily endorse the settlement that you've generated in mediation. California courts are crowded, and judges want you to help yourself. They simply don't have the time to become intimately familiar with every aspect of your life. No one is better qualified to make decisions about your divorce than you and your spouse.

Warren Burger, former Chief Justice of the United States Supreme Court, hailed divorce mediation as "the Brave New World of settling marital disputes." Indeed, mediation has several distinct advantages when compared to the traditional adversarial divorce process. Not only does it typically cost much less, it also allows individuals to retain complete control over the divorce process. Instead of relying on a court (or aggressive attorneys) to make decisions that will impact them for years to come, individuals in mediation control the outcome of their own divorce proceedings. An added benefit is that a marital separation agreement that springs from mediation is more likely to be honored than an agreement that is forced upon both parties after litigation.

How Mediation Works

Simply put, a mediator's job is to maximize a couple's chance of reaching a satisfactory settlement. A mediator will neither represent you nor your spouse. Instead, he or she will work closely with both of you to negotiate a legally binding divorce agreement. To reach that goal, a mediator often guides clients through five stages. The stages typically progress in sequential order, but some issues may require looping back to earlier stages. The five stages are:

1) Introductory
2) Information Gathering
3) Framing
4) Negotiating
5) Concluding

Introductory

During the introductory session, the mediator will explain how the mediation sessions will be conducted. Beyond simply discussing the overall structure of the mediation sessions, the mediator will give you the opportunity to present background information about your particular situation. In addition, you will have the opportunity to ask any questions you have about the mediation process.

Information Gathering

During the information gathering stage, the mediator will begin the important process of helping you gather and organize information pertinent to your divorce.

This may include collecting tax returns, bank and mortgage statements, W-2s, information about insurance policies (medical, life, auto), and financial information regarding other investments or family businesses. The mediator's overriding goal is to ensure that you and your spouse have access to all of the facts you need to negotiate a binding and satisfactory settlement.

Framing

Determining and understanding each spouse's reason for desiring a certain outcome is a critical part of the mediation process. These concerns, goals, priorities and values are generally referred to as "interests," and they form the backbone of the negotiating phase. In some instances, the interests of both spouses will overlap nicely, which greatly eases the challenge of reaching settlement on that particular issue. By the end of the framing stage, each spouse should not only understand the issues that require negotiation, but should also be aware of the other spouse's underlying interests.

Negotiating

During this stage, the spouses discuss various options that may lead to settlement. The mediator helps the spouses articulate options that best address their respective interests. Sometimes couples need to start with a small issue to "warm up" before tackling big issues (such as child custody or spousal support), while other couples are ready to jump straight into the most contentious issue. Each mediator handles the negotiation stage differently, but most mediators will help you weed out clearly unacceptable options before focusing on promising alternatives. The spouses will consider how they may compromise on certain issues in order to ensure that their interests are fully satisfied with regard to other issues.

Concluding

At this point, an attorney-mediator will often translate your tentative settlement into a legally binding agreement that can be filed with the court. A non-attorney mediator is not permitted to draft the marital separation agreement, and as a result, the mediator will likely enlist the services of an attorney for this task. In most instances, a mediator will require that each spouse consult briefly with another attorney who only represents him or her before signing the marital separation agreement. This ensures that both spouses enjoy the benefit of an experienced attorney's analysis of their settlement before filing it in court, which only further bolsters its enforceability.

Picking a Mediator

It could be that a friend of yours has used a mediator and had a positive experience. Referrals are always a great way to find a good mediator. If, like many Californians, you don't know anyone who has used a mediator, you can simply interview a few and decide whom you like the best. Most mediators maintain a webpage; a simple on-line search for mediators can be a good starting point. Here are a few qualities to look for:

Training

A mediator should have completed at least one 40-hour program in mediation. This is hardly enough to signal competency, but it's a start. Some attorneys feel that because they have experience as family lawyers, mediation training isn't necessary. This simply is not true. Mediation and litigation are two entirely different processes with vastly different skill sets. Indeed, some wonderful litigators make horrible mediators. Likewise, while I consider myself a good mediator, I would not make a particularly good litigator. Mediation training teaches students to approach divorce differently. Instead of arguing over positions, you learn to uncover underlying interests. It sounds simple, but it actually takes some training to develop the tools to get this done effectively.

Experience

A more experienced mediator is a better mediator, right? Often, but not always. Certainly you should seek a mediator who has more than a few mediations under his or her belt, but once the threshold of competency has been passed, personality and style are more important than number of cases mediated. Very experienced mediators will cost more, and they may not have as much time to devote to your case. On the other hand, their experience may help them deal with complex financial situations, unusual custodial arrangements, and high conflict mediation sessions.

Style

Each mediator brings his or her own personal style to a mediation, ranging from extremely passive to fairly aggressive. At one extreme, a mediator may simply make arrangements for the parties (and potentially their attorneys, if they are represented) to meet in a neutral location, and then utter scarcely a word. At the other extreme, a mediator may strongly advocate for a certain position he or she feels is the best alternative for the parties. Most clients prefer an approach somewhere between the two.

Some mediators focus almost exclusively on interpreting, reframing, and paraphrasing the parties' comments in an attempt to help them communicate more clearly, while others will actively work with the parties to generate and expand options for settlement. Some mediators will attempt to predict the position a judge would take on a particular issue, while others think such speculation is inappropriate.

In short, mediators use a wide variety of styles. There is no right or wrong answer, though anything at the extremes demands a bit more scrutiny. You should pick a mediator whose approach to mediation makes you comfortable.

<u>Critical Qualities</u>

Above all else, you must trust your mediator and have absolute faith in his or her integrity. Beyond that simple requirement, you should also look for a mediator who exhibits some of the following qualities: common sense, empathy, creativity, flexibility, humor, intelligence, and optimism. Decide which of these qualities is most important to you, and don't settle for a mediator who doesn't exemplify your priorities. Also, don't hesitate to decline working with a mediator simply because he or she makes you uncomfortable. For mediation to succeed, you must intuitively feel that you are working with a nonjudgmental, fair, and unbiased professional.

Attorney v. Other Professional

Who makes the best mediator—a therapist, an attorney, or a financial professional? While many mediators are attorneys, some mediators are mental health professionals or financial advisors.

Divorce has an emotional component, a financial component, and a legal component. A therapist will be well versed in addressing the first of these components. A financial planner will be well versed in addressing the second. A lawyer is the only party who may address the third. When I first started working as a divorce mediator, I was under the misguided impression that hiring an attorney-mediator was the most sensible approach for nearly any divorcing couple, as an attorney-mediator is the only professional who can tackle all three components of a divorce. Years later, I have come to the realization that this is often simply not true.

Understanding why therapists can make outstanding mediators doesn't take much of an intellectual leap of faith. After all, therapists receive extensive training in active listening and reframing, two of the key skills utilized in mediation, and they tend to be skilled at diffusing emotionally charged situations. Contrast these qualities with the skill set that is celebrated in law school, and the challenge that attorney-mediators face becomes clear. Law school teaches budding attorneys to act as advocates – i.e., to tirelessly pursue the best possible result for *one* client. Keeping the best interests of *both* clients in mind while acting as a neutral third party involves a very different set of skills.

Keep in mind that drafting a strong a marital separation agreement that adequately protects the rights of each spouse is wrapped in legal complexity and requires advanced legal drafting skills. If you are drawn to the idea of using a therapist-mediator but worry that he or she won't be able to "get you to the finish line" (i.e., complete your divorce) because this final critical step requires the help of a lawyer, I suggest that you simply find a therapist-mediator who works closely with a reputable divorce attorney. Indeed, this is the model that has been embraced by all of the California Divorce Mediation therapist-mediators.

Part-time v. Full-time Attorney Mediators

Many lawyers advertise their services as a mediator, when in reality the vast majority of their caseload comes from litigation. Other lawyers have made a conscious decision to restrict their legal practice to mediation alone. While mediators who also litigate family law cases may be intimately familiar with the intricacies of the local court system, they may be overloaded with conflicting deadlines and client demands. In addition, the part-time mediator may not have the time to focus on mediator-specific training, an important component of competency. Lastly, an attorney who offers mediation as an add-on service faces the considerable challenge of shifting from an aggressive litigation-oriented mindset to the facilitative mindset of a mediator. This is analogous to an instantaneous transformation from gladiator to peacemaker. It's a tough transition, and it takes a special lawyer to do it successfully.

Co-mediation

Partnerships between therapists and attorneys in mediation have worked well in many instances. The therapist typically focuses on improving communication and dealing with underlying emotional conflict, while the attorney helps provide a legal backdrop for discussions. The therapist may be particularly skilled at dealing with issues such as co-parenting, while the attorney may be well versed in the law surrounding such issues as spousal support, child support, and property division.

Some mediation teams are also gender-balanced (meaning they consist of one male and one female), and while this makes some clients more comfortable, concerns of gender bias are typically unfounded. Most mediators have received extensive training in maintaining neutrality. That said, receiving the benefit of two perspectives on a particular situation can be refreshing.

Co-mediation, while offering the combined skills of two professionals, also presents challenges of its own. Quite frankly, some co-mediation teams just don't work particularly well together, and they may speak over each other or even offer conflicting advice. In addition, co-mediation tends to be more expensive than mediating with a single professional.

Co-mediation has advantages and drawbacks, but if you and your spouse find that working with a team helps you navigate the divorce process more effectively, it's a possibility worth considering. Most major metropolitan areas offer several attorney/therapist teams; one of them may provide the perfect balance for your own divorce.

Communication During Mediation

Good communication is the key to successful mediation. Indeed, much of a mediator's job involves getting both parties to communicate clearly and effectively. When you begin the mediation process, the flow of communication between you and your spouse may have reached rock bottom. Learning to communicate effectively amidst the emotionally-charged atmosphere of divorce can be difficult, but it is absolutely essential.

Any verbal statement consists of two parts: (1) the speaker's intended statement, and (2) the listener's interpretation of that statement. When the two don't align, problems arise. Both the speaker and the listener carry their own responsibilities.

Being a Good Speaker

The speaker must work on stating his or her intention clearly. What is it that the speaker wants to convey? Simple factual information? Or perhaps disagreement or anger? If you are speaking and your message has emotional content, don't be afraid to say so. "What you just said makes me angry," is a perfectly valid comment. On the other hand, something like, "You spend over $1,000 a month on clothing!" delivered with scorn, may just be an attack masked as a factual statement. Instead, try, "I feel that a clothing allowance of $1,000 a month is too much." You're clearly stating your concern, opening the door to discussion instead of a pointed rebuke.

The speaker has to be very careful to avoid statements laden with blame during mediation. Blaming the other party for some perceived wrongdoing is a surefire way to either (1) ensure that the other party stops listening, or (2) prompt a counterattack. This doesn't mean that you can't say anything about your spouse or your spouse's behavior. It simply means that if you do so, you should phrase your concern carefully.

Using "I" statements instead of "you" statements is a good way to ensure that communication stays productive. People naturally respond defensively to the use of the word "you" in a negative or even slightly critical context. Try rephrasing expressions of concern using your own feelings as the starting point. For instance, instead of saying, "You never pay the bills on time, and you've screwed up our credit," try, "I'm concerned that our credit report is negatively affected by late payments." The first statement sets the speaker up for a defensive response, whereas the second statement comes across as something a bit closer to neutral.

Some more examples of "you" and corresponding "I" statements:

You	"You always run up huge credit card bills, and now you're making it impossible for me to pay the rent."
I	"I'm concerned about how I am going to pay the rent with such a large credit card balance."
You	"You are never there for our kids. You've always been absent."
I	"I'd like to figure out how you can spend more time with the kids. I'm concerned that they don't see you enough."
You	"You were late picking up the kids last week, and because of you, Haley missed her ballet practice."
I	"It really bothered me that you picked up Haley late last week. Her ballet practice starts at 3pm. Will you be able to get her there on time this week?"

You	"You shouldn't spend so much on cars. Your list of expenses is way too high. We're getting divorced, and you'll have to cut back on your hobby."
I	"I'd like to figure out how we can both budget effectively and stretch our income. I feel like trimming discretionary expenses like hobbies might be a good place to start."

Many people instinctively state a solution immediately after raising a problem. This is not a good tactic in mediation. The solution to the problem may seem obvious, and it may be just waiting there on the tip of your tongue. Because it's so obvious, surely your spouse will acknowledge that you are correct, right? Again, don't do it. Mediation is successful when parties work together to come up with a solution to a problem. Present the problem and then let your spouse think about it for a while. Once discussions have started, you can gently insert your idea. But in the meantime, really listen to what your spouse has to say. You may be surprised by an idea you hadn't considered.

Being a Good Listener

While the speaker is responsible for presenting information as accurately and fairly as possible, the listener has an equally important job—really listening. Listening well requires being present, something far too many of us fail to honor. The tendency to stop listening and start formulating a rebuttal once we detect a note of criticism in the speaker's voice is natural. Just remember that listening and agreeing are not the same thing. Let the speaker finish his or her statement, and acknowledge that you will have plenty of time to disagree when he or she is finished. A term that is often used to describe this process of mentally interrupting the words that reach your ears is "self-listening." Try to avoid letting your own thoughts obscure what the other party is trying to convey.

Beyond avoiding self-listening, a good listener doesn't make quick assumptions about the speaker's message. This is particularly difficult in mediation, because most spouses in mediation are intimately familiar with the other's speech patterns, facial expressions, and tones of voice. You might think, "I've seen that look before. Here it comes!" Anything that follows that thought won't truly be heard. You may think you can read your spouse's mind (and you may be right some of the time), but by truly listening and refraining from making assumptions, you will aid the mediation process and ensure that you understand your spouse's concerns.

Mediation v. Litigation – an Illustration

To illustrate how mediation differs from litigation, consider the following scenarios. In the first example I assume the role of divorce litigator. In the second, I act in my chosen capacity, as a divorce mediator.

Jessica and Steve – The Litigated Divorce

Jessica walks into my office. She greets me with a firm handshake and fire in her eyes. A middle-aged brunette, she is dressed in a crisp suit, suggesting that she is a white-collar worker. She squares her shoulders, takes a deep breath, and before I can ask her to sit down, she explains that yesterday she received an unwelcome delivery at work—divorce papers!

"It was embarrassing!" Jessica exclaims. "I am a vice president at a large public company. All of my co-workers watched as some guy shoved a bunch of legal forms in my face. And worst of all, the paperwork kindly informed me that I was prohibited from hiding assets. Hiding assets! As if I don't make all of the money in this relationship!"

I ask to review her paperwork. After examining the documents she received, I discover that her husband, Steve, has retained the services of Chris Watkins, one of the most notoriously difficult divorce attorneys around. This is not good news.

I learn that Mr. Watkins has already set a temporary hearing to determine how support and custody of their two young children will be handled while the divorce is pending. That means that I only have a few weeks to learn everything I need to know about Jessica and Steve, their finances, their parenting styles, their needs, their shortcomings.

The general approach that Mr. Watkins will take on Steve's behalf quickly becomes apparent—grab as much as possible as quickly as possible. Steve works part-time as a fitness instructor, and he contributes approximately $30,000 per year to the marriage. He also spends significantly more time with the children than Jessica, who works 50 hours a week and brings home $250,000 per year. The support that Mr. Watkins seeks for Steve is more than Jessica's income justifies, and worse yet, he wants Jessica to move out of the house until the divorce is finalized.

Jessica is terrified that the court will grant custody of the children to Steve, and that her involvement in parenting will be relegated to "visits" every other weekend. Her eyes moisten as she describes how she works as hard as she does for her kids, and that if her work is used against her in a divorce, she'll be devastated. She also expresses disbelief that Steve, who had been a loving, supportive husband for eight years, has suddenly decided to leave her without any warning.

"What if he is cheating on me?" Jessica asks. She pauses, corrects herself, "Of course he is cheating on me! That's the only explanation. Can I use that against him?"

I explain to Jessica that California is a no-fault state, and that a judge won't be concerned about the reasons Steve wants a divorce.

"What can we use against him, then? He can definitely make way more than he does. After all, the guy has a degree from UCSD."

Jessica has already slipped into the classic adversarial mindset. Her husband is "coming after her," and she is going to fight back with everything she can muster. It's my job to help her.

"A judge could impute income to Steve, but that depends on a number of variables," I say. "Did he ever do anything besides work as a fitness instructor?"

"He was an investment banker!" Jessica exclaims. "Until we had kids, he pulled down a huge salary. I became his meal ticket."

I record this bit of ammunition on my legal pad and immediately start to think tactically. I need financial information, and I need it fast. Temporary support for Steve will largely be based on routine calculations, but the judge will have a certain amount of discretion, and I want to walk into the temporary support hearing well prepared.

Jessica and I begin to pick Steve apart. We analyze his spending, coming up with a low-ball figure for his everyday needs. We also talk to Jessica and Steve's broker, and we discover that Steve sold a number of shares of stock just before filing for divorce, the proceeds from which are now sitting in his separate bank account. Presumably he is using the funds to pay Mr. Watkins for his services. We also discover that Steve ran up massive credit card debt in the month prior to filing for divorce. Some of the charges are for expensive dinners, and it appears that several thousand dollars were spent on a supposed "camping retreat" with the guys.

Steve's financial irresponsibility is the subject of much discussion, but his former drug use is the jackpot. To ensure that Jessica gets plenty of custody, we'll need to show that Steve is unfit to be a single parent. I sense that Steve's drug use (cocaine, back in his investment banker days) was a passing phase, and that he is now clean, but if needed, we can trot out that piece of information to our advantage.

Jessica and I spend hours preparing for the hearing. Unsurprisingly, the judge simply uses a formula to calculate the amount that Jessica will have to pay Steve. It's a bigger number than we had hoped for, but it's manageable, and post-divorce support is what really concerns us.

Following the hearing, Mr. Watkins and I speak on the phone with increasing frequency. We both know we'll settle the case before trial, but we are posturing, constantly searching for an advantage that might sway a court in our favor. We talk about Steve's financial habits, his suspicious transfers prior to filing for divorce, and the allegations that Jessica doesn't have the capacity for more than 20% custody.

Jessica has meanwhile become very familiar with the fact that child support in California is tied to a statutory formula, and that the time-share percentage plays a huge role in determining the amount of support that must be paid. Mr. Watkins has advised Steve not to communicate with Jessica, which naturally makes her constantly second-guess Steve's intentions. She comes to my office breathing fire, determined to whittle down Steve's custody as much as possible. She claims she simply wants more time with her children, and while I know this is partially true, her real motivation is becoming apparent. She simply wants to limit that amount of child support she is forced to pay. This is no surprise to me—this attitude is routine in litigated divorces—so I tell her that I'll do everything I can.

The issue of Steve's former drug use becomes heated. In response to Jessica's allegations that Steve has battled drug addiction and shouldn't be given custody of the children, Steve's lawyer drops a bombshell of his own. Apparently Jessica has dabbled in drugs as well. She never told me this. I confront her about this piece of information, and she sheepishly admits that she occasionally smokes pot with a co-worker. She doesn't know how this information got into Steve's hands. She was always very careful to cover her tracks. Besides, she insists, pot is no big deal.

I inform her that we've suffered a major setback. At this point I know Jessica fairly well. Her love for her children is genuine, she is a responsible working mom, and she simply wants to come out of this divorce process in one piece. Now that Mr. Watkins knows she has a pot habit, he can paint an ugly picture of Jessica's parenting ability. Not only does she see the kids less frequently than Steve, she is also recreational drug user. This is going to be a battle.

Both Mr. Watkins and I spend time tearing into the financial disclosures prepared by each of our clients. I assert that Steve has padded his budget to cover the cost of luxury goods, and that his "entertainment" line item is absurd. I speculate that most of the entertainment budget consists of money spent on his lover. Mr. Watkins backs down, and then counterattacks by questioning the number my client has attributed to "business clothing." He can barely contain the scorn in his voice as he discusses Jessica's expensive taste in clothes.

Steve's physical training practice, while relatively modest, is still an asset. Valuing the practice is no small task. I hire an appraiser whom I know will generously value the practice. My thinking is straightforward: the more valuable Steve's practice, the more concessions we can demand in exchange for letting him keep it.

I am also prepared to show that Steve could easily join the mainstream workforce and earn many times what he earns today. I don't particularly care that Steve feels that physical training is his calling. I care that he used to make six figures as an investment banker, and now he is trying to squeeze excessive spousal support out of my client. To make my point, I hire a career placement expert who will happily testify that Steve has great income potential.

Steve and Jessica have taken a backseat in their own divorce. Mr. Watkins and I negotiate endlessly, using a predicable offer/counter-offer approach that has each of us requesting concessions and granting them in return. We dutifully run our offers past our clients, but we are firmly in control of the process. Eventually we settle on a number for spousal support that neither favors Steve nor Jessica. (In fact, we could have arrived at the same number months ago, but we were both busy trading concessions. We came full circle, at a huge cost to our clients).

My legal bill combined with expert fees has now climbed past $50,000, and we haven't settled yet. Steve's lawyer and I are having a hard time coming to an agreement with regard to division of the family home. I don't feel that Steve should be entitled to continue living in the home simply because he has carried more of the childrearing responsibility in the relationship. Indeed, I know that the house is the couple's biggest asset, and I am not about to give this up. If anything, I will force a sale.

Mr. Watkins and I are both thinking strategically, carefully calculating what we might be able to get away with in court. Because we are both tenacious attorneys, we are warily circling each other, unable to stomach the thought of "losing" any particular point.

In the meantime, the couple's children are starting to act out. In accordance with the temporary custody arrangement, and at his attorney's suggestion, Steve has requested that they "hand off" the children at a neutral location—in this case, the local library. Jessica can't bear to be near Steve, nor can he bear to be near her. The kids feel the tension deeply, and they feel pulled in two directions. Their son has started bullying other children at school, while their daughter has become increasingly sullen and withdrawn.

Jessica looks a mess. My fees have eaten up a nice piece of her nest egg, and all she knows is that (1) she is being forced to pay a huge amount of money to her husband while she waits for the lawyers to reach a settlement, (2) she doesn't get to see her children as often as she would like, and (3) she feels like she's constantly under attack. The feistiness that marked her initial appearance in my office is gone. She is still angry, but she looks defeated.

And yet we've only just begun.

A full year later, the divorce is finalized. Several reams of paper, hundreds of attorney hours, several expert witness consultations, and countless spilled tears later, Jessica is a single woman. The total cost of her divorce, including my fees, expert fees, and Mr. Watkins' fees, comes to $140,000. The emotional cost is even higher. Jessica and Steve detest each other, and they have trouble communicating about their children. The result of all of the negotiating is predictable: child support payments in accordance with the statutory guidelines, spousal support that isn't a victory or defeat for Jessica, and a custodial arrangement that grants her slightly less custody than she would like.

Jessica and Steve – The Mediated Divorce

Steve calls me late in the afternoon. He says he wants a divorce, but he hasn't yet told his wife, Jessica. He wants to know how to get through the process as painlessly as possible. I inform him that mediation is a good approach, as it ensures that both parties to the divorce have their needs addressed at a reasonable cost. I also tell him, firmly, that both spouses have to agree to mediate, and that he needs to discuss his plans with his wife. If she agrees to mediate, I will help them.

One week later Steve calls me again. He says that he told Jessica about his desire for a divorce, and it didn't go well. She stuffed a suitcase full of clothes and fled to a friend's house. Jessica's friends are telling her to hire an aggressive divorce attorney, but after reading a bit about mediation, she is willing to meet with me.

The following week Jessica knocks on my door. I offer her a cup of coffee and ask her to take a seat. Shifting nervously, she asks me if I represent her husband. I tell her that I don't represent either of them. My role is to help them separate in a manner that best meets their respective needs and minimizes the inevitable emotional and financial strain of divorce. I begin to wonder if she is an attorney as she grills me on my credentials. Satisfied that I know what I'm talking about, she seems to relax.

Steve walks in moments later. He visibly cringes at the sight of his wife, as if he expects her to reach out and slap him across the face. Jessica's arms immediately cross over her chest as she glares at her husband.

I escort them both from my waiting room to my conference room, and we each take a seat at the round table. I spend the next ten minutes explaining how I work. I emphasize the importance of clear communication, full disclosure, and respect. It's clear to me that Steve and Jessica are having a hard time focusing on the words coming from my mouth. Anger, distrust, and guilt saturate the room.

As soon as I begin to wind up my explanation of how mediation works, Jessica looks at Steve and blurts, "I can't believe you're sleeping with Cindy! What is wrong with you? Do you think you're going to do better than me? You think that tramp has something to offer?"

Steve sits immobile, wide-eyed, clearly unable to respond.

I step in. "Jessica, it's clear to me that you're upset about the prospect of getting divorced. I sense that this was a surprise to you."

"You could say that again," Jessica says. "I never saw this coming. Not in a million years."

I look at Steve, then Jessica. "Have you considered marital counseling? Are you certain that divorce is the answer?"

Steve looks down. "I don't want to go to counseling. This is what I want. I'm done with this marriage."

"You're done?" Jessica asks, her anger giving way to tears. "We have kids together! Please, Steve."

Steve merely shakes his head. "I want out. I don't want to be married to you anymore."

Jessica looks at me in disbelief. "Just like that. Can you believe it? Just like that..."

Couples who have long contemplated divorce tend to settle easily into the mediation process. They know divorce is coming, and they have had time to digest the reality of separation. Steve and Jessica present a more challenging case. Jessica feels blindsided by the news that her husband wants out. It will take her some time to accept the unpleasant reality that her life is about to change dramatically.

"Jessica," I say, "you haven't had any time to digest the news that Steve wants to end your marriage. We aren't going to make any big decisions today, but I'd like to know about your current living arrangements. Where are you staying?"

Steve, Jessica and I discuss their current predicament. Jessica is staying at a friend's house, and while it's been less than a week, she can't bear being away from her children. Steve softens visibly at this confession. He reassures Jessica that her role as the mother of their children is something he values highly. He wants her to see the kids.

After half an hour of discussion, and a few more tears, Steve and Jessica have come to a temporary agreement. Jessica will move back into the master bedroom. Steve will move into the guest room, and they will meet together with their two children, aged six and eight, to discuss what is unfolding. They agree to come back in a week. In the meantime, I email them my mediation agreement and ask them to bring signed copies to our next meeting.

The following week Steve and Jessica reappear in my office. They are still frosty toward each other, but Jessica's anger has been replaced by a business-like demeanor that reflects her employment as a technology company executive. While she may not want a divorce, she seems to understand that Steve is committed to proceeding. She wants to get down to business.

Although normally I would move into information gathering at this point, I sense that Steve and Jessica may need assistance sorting out how the separation process will work. As we discuss interim living arrangements, Jessica explains that she will be moving into a nearby apartment. She wants to jump into a discussion of what will ultimately happen to the house, but I suggest that we delay that discussion until we've pulled all of their financial information together. At this point I don't know if avoiding a sale of the home is a possibility.

My first priority is ensuring that the both Steve and Jessica have access to the children. I prompt them to come up with a workable schedule until we reach a solid custody arrangement. Because Jessica works long hours and Steve spends a great deal of time at home, they agree that Jessica will have the children from Friday evening to Monday morning every other week and will take the children to dinner every Wednesday night. Steve has also agreed that Jessica may put the kids to bed in their home on Wednesday evenings as well.

With a temporary custody arrangement behind us, I walk Steve and Jessica through the information gathering process. I give them a comprehensive list of data and financial statements they need to provide, then send them on their way. We will review what they have collected during our next meeting. I also ask them to fill out income and expense reports.

Two weeks later we are all sitting in my office again, pouring over financial information. The process is greatly streamlined by the fact that Jessica religiously uses accounting software for their home finances, and has diligently kept track of their expenses. This is good news, but it also means that Jessica is much more familiar with the family finances than Steve. I will have to work to ensure that Steve is fully informed regarding any financial decisions.

We quickly realize (as is almost always the case) that the couple's combined income isn't sufficient to maintain the standard of living that they've grown accustomed to enjoying. Maintaining two households is simply much more expensive that maintaining one, a truth that all divorcing couples must face. Something must give. This is when the negotiations get heated.

We review their respective expense reports. Steve, normally low-key and docile, starts to get agitated.

"What in the world is this crap?" he asks. "Five hundred dollars a month for clothes? You have got to be kidding me! Give me a break!"

I remind Steve about our rules regarding maintaining a respectful tone, then turn to Jessica and ask her if she thinks she can trim her clothing expenses.

"Not a chance," she says, arms crossed. "After all, it's my money. I bring home all of the cash around here, so I have a right to spend it."

I remind Jessica that we're not fixating on who has a right to spend what, but rather how we can use their existing resources to best meet both of their needs.

"Well, then, what the heck is this?" Jessica asks, pointing to a line item in Steve's report. It shows seven hundred dollars a month in entertainment expenses.

"I need to get out once in a while!" Steve protests. "I don't get to live it up like you do during your so-called 'business travel'."

"Live it up?" Jessica is standing now, her voice shaking. "You think that all of those days on the road are fun? What is wrong with you?"

Time to de-escalate a bit. The temperature in the room is getting way too high for constructive dialogue. I stop them both, guide them to my break room for a drink of water. The two of them avoid each other studiously. I debate whether caucusing would be more effective at this point. Caucusing simply involves meeting with each spouse separately. It has a clear advantage—minimizing outbursts and facilitating clearer thinking—but it also has a disadvantage. Spouses sometimes fear that the mediator is secretly sympathizing with the other. Even when complete impartiality is maintained (as it should be), the spouses may struggle with the concept.

I decide to keep them together and avoid caucusing for the time being. I direct their attention to the facts. They have a set amount of monthly income, and they will have to figure out how to provide not just one home for their children, but two. Each will have to make sacrifices. We start to dig deeper into the interests behind each spouse's listed expenses. Once Jessica clearly expresses that her clothing is an important part of her professional image, and that her professional image helps bring home a high salary, Steve starts to back down. And when Jessica senses that Steve understands her true interest in her stated clothing expenses, she thinks out loud about how she could reduce her expenses.

"I might be able to trim $100 a month from that budget," Jessica states. "I wouldn't like it, but I could do it."

Steve nods. "And I could reduce my entertainment expenses a bit. It's just that I realize I won't have the kids every night, and I'd like to be able to do things."

Suddenly Jessica looks like she is about to cry. She looks away. Steve gently touches her arm, and she pulls away.

"Steve, how much do you think you can trim from your entertainment budget?" I ask.

"Maybe I could get away with $400 a month," he says "That might work."

"You're both making progress," I say. "In the last two minutes you've managed to trim $400 from your monthly expenses."

"Yay," Jessica says sarcastically, sniffing to hold back the tears. "Only $2600 to go."

I remind them that while trimming expenses is the best way to ensure that maintaining two houses is feasible, some couples achieve the same result by finding additional income.

Jessica raises an eyebrow and simply gives Steve *the look*.

"I'm not going back into investment banking," he says quickly. "Besides, they wouldn't take me back. It's been too long. Once you're out, you're out."

"Is there something else you could do with your financial background that might bring in more money?" I ask.

Jessica reminds him, "You still have a ton of friends in the financial sector, and you are recognized for your expertise in the healthcare field. You could consult."

"Maybe," Steve says. "Not full time, but maybe part time."

"How much could you expect to make consulting part time?" I ask.

"Sixty grand, minimum," Jessica interjects.

"I'd like to hear what Steve thinks," I say.

Steve shrugs. "She's probably right. Sixty grand, maybe."

I nod, happy at this change of direction. "That's great. Even accounting for taxes, that's a huge boost to your income. That alone might cover the cost of maintaining a second home."

"Well?" Jessica asks.

"I could teach a few fitness classes a week, and also consult. But our childcare expenses would go up," Steve said. "That's going to be really expensive. I'm usually home with the kids. That would be a big change."

"How much do you think childcare would cost?" I ask.

"Let's be real," Jessica says. "Our kids are in school. If they aren't busy with after-school activities, they can stay with my mom. During the summers they can go to day camp. It wouldn't be that expensive."

Steve closes his eyes. A moment later he opens them and says, "Okay."

"Okay?" Jessica asks.

"I said, 'Okay,'" Steve repeats. "I'll look into it. But only if you're fair about splitting our assets."

"I'm not out to screw you," Jessica says. "I just want to be fair. After all, this divorce is your idea."

Steve agrees to start making phone calls about prospective jobs ("lighting up his network" is what he calls it). The tension in the room is dissipating quickly, and the session ultimately ends on a positive note.

Fast forward one month. Jessica and Steve have sorted out the financial aspect of their divorce. Jessica has agreed to let Steve keep the house in exchange for (1) waiving spousal support, and (2) a modest cash payment. Jessica has moved into a three-bedroom home not far from Steve and agreed to a reasonable figure for child support.

The temporary custody arrangement is working well, and Steve and Jessica agree to incorporate it into their marital separation agreement. They also include the caveat that they will revisit the issue of custody in two years. Although Jessica is still very angry with Steve, she has managed to preserve a civil relationship with him for the sake of their children. All of the substantive negotiation is done. Jessica and Steve now simply have to wait a few months until their divorce is final. A judge will most assuredly honor their marital separation agreement.

All told, Jessica and Steve have saved more than a hundred thousand dollars and preserved a cordial relationship by mediating their divorce. This result may seem startling, but it's not at all unusual. Doing things the grownup way has enormous benefits.

CHAPTER 3

The Divorce Process, Step by Step

"The nuts and bolts"

Keep in mind that if you use an attorney or a divorce mediator to help you with your divorce, he or she will guide you through all of the steps listed below and will most likely prepare all of the required documents for you. Nevertheless, it's a good idea to have a basic understanding of the divorce process, from the initial filing to the final judgment. Many self-help books are intended to provide a detailed look at all of the necessary forms required for a "do-it-yourself" divorce. This is not one of them. The following simply provides an overview of how the process works in California for a non-litigated divorce.

Once you've decided to divorce, you will need to file some basic documents with the clerk of the court for the county in which you live. Understand that even if you mediate your divorce or have otherwise come to an agreement with your spouse regarding property division, support, and custody, one of you will still have to "sue" the other. Clients often balk at this process, but it's simply the way the system works. Remember, while you avoid much of the adversarial system by acting like a grownup, you are stuck with the procedural trappings of the local courts.

Step 1:

Determine where you should file for divorce. If you have resided in (1) California for the past six months and (2) the same county for the past three months, the answer is simple. File in the county where you currently reside.

Step 2:

Decide if (1) you or (2) your spouse is going to file for divorce. Understand that this has no special significance in California. Initiating divorce does not somehow put you at a disadvantage. The one of you who decides to file is called the "Petitioner."

Step 3:

The Petitioner (let's assume you are the Petitioner) must fill out Family Law Form 100 (FL-100), otherwise known as the "Petition." This form requires basic information, such as your date of marriage, your date of separation, the names and birthdates of your children, whether you are seeking a legal separation or a divorce, and whether your decision to divorce or separate is based on "irreconcilable differences" or "incurable insanity." Needless to say, "irreconcilable differences" is the appropriate choice 99% of the time. You will also need to check several boxes with regard to the relief you are requesting from the court (i.e., whether you want the court to determine your property rights, who should receive custody of the children, etc.).

Step 4:

You, the Petitioner, must complete Family Law Form 110 (FL-110), otherwise known as the "Summons." The Summons is a basic document that serves to notify your spouse (i.e., the "Respondent") that you have filed for divorce. The Summons is simple to complete.

Step 5:

If you and your spouse have children together, you must fill out Family Law Form 105 (FL-105), otherwise known as the "Declaration Under Uniform Child Custody Jurisdiction and Enforcement Act" ("UCCJEA form"). This form simply contains information regarding your children and where they have lived for the past five years (at a minimum), as well as some basic questions about potential custody complications (such as restraining orders, other court proceedings involving the children, etc.).

Step 6:

Depending on the rules of your local court, you may need to complete one or more additional local forms to file for divorce. For instance, at the time of the writing of this book, Santa Clara County requires a "Declaration of Residence." San Mateo County, on the other hand, currently requires a form titled, "The San Mateo County Superior Court recommends ADR options." If you are completing divorce paperwork yourself, simply check the website of the county where you will file, or call the county clerk to determine what local forms must be completed.

Step 7:

You, the Petitioner, file the Petition, the Summons, the UCCJEA form, and any required local forms at the county courthouse. If your forms have been completed properly, the clerk will stamp the documents and assign a case number and judge. If you made a mistake, the clerk will typically point out the problem so you can generate a new form.

Step 8:

You, the Petitioner, must ensure that your spouse is "served" with the Summons, the Petition, the UCCJEA form (if applicable), a blank response, and a blank UCCJEA form. This can be done in a variety of ways, from hiring a third party to hand deliver the documents to your spouse to mailing the documents to your spouse yourself. A mediator will often deliver the Summons to your spouse for you.

If you have a third party hand deliver the documents, he or she will need to complete and sign a form titled "Proof of Personal Service" (FL-330). If you opted to mail the forms to your spouse, you should complete a form titled, "Proof of Service by Mail" (FL-335).

Note that once your spouse has been served with your divorce paperwork, the following restraining orders come into effect, and you and your spouse are prohibited from taking the following actions without the written consent of the other:

Standard Family Law Restraining Orders
1. Removing the minor child or children of the parties, if any, from the state without the prior written consent of the other party or an order of the court;
2. Cashing, borrowing against, canceling, transferring, disposing of, or changing the beneficiaries of any insurance or other coverage, including life, health, automobile, and disability, held for the benefit of the parties and their minor child or children;
3. Transferring, encumbering, hypothecating, concealing, or in any way disposing of any property, real or personal, whether community, quasi-community, or separate, without the written consent of the other party or an order of the court, except in the usual course of business or for the necessities of life; and
4. Creating a nonprobate transfer or modifying a nonprobate transfer in a manner that affects the disposition of property subject to the transfer, without the written consent of the other party of an order of

> the court. Before revocation of a nonprobate transfer can take effect or a right of survivorship to property can be eliminated, notice of the change must be filed and served on the other party.

Some of these restraining orders are easy to decipher. Others take a bit of work. Keep in mind that to "hypothecate" an asset simply means to allow a lender to place a lien on the asset—in other words, to make it collateral for an obligation. Also, note that a "nonprobate" transfer is simply a transfer that falls outside of the probate process (i.e., the process that governs the disposition of your assets upon death). For example, if you hold title to your home as joint tenants with your spouse, the transfer of full title to your spouse upon your death is considered a nonprobate transfer. Therefore, severing the joint tenancy on your home is one example of a nonprobate transfer that would require that you file a notice with the clerk and serve the notice on your spouse.

Step 9:

Next, both you and your spouse must complete a number of financial disclosure forms. It is extremely important that you fill out all of the financial disclosure forms as thoroughly and accurately as possible. If you don't, your spouse may have reason to re-visit your divorce settlement years down the road. The courts rightfully place a great deal of emphasis on full disclosure of financial assets.

The Income and Expense Declaration (FL-150) will take a great deal of thought, and you should use the utmost care in completing it. Not only does the form require details about your education, sources of income, assets, and deductions, it also requires a detailed breakdown of your monthly expenses, including such items as groceries, utility bills, telephone expenses, childcare, clothes, education, insurance, auto expenses, and uninsured healthcare costs. This information plays an important role in any support-related negotiation (including mediation). As always, the "act like a grownup" adage applies. Fill out your forms accurately and fairly, and you will greatly ease the divorce process. Overinflate expenses to create an inaccurate picture of your living requirements and you will simply open the door to litigation.

The Schedule of Assets and Debts (FL-142) likewise requires your full attention and should be filled out as accurately as possible. You will be required to list all of your assets, including real estate, household furniture, jewelry, art, antiques, vehicles, savings accounts, cash, investment accounts, unsecured notes, retirement plans and pensions, etc.

One you have completed these two forms, you must deliver them to your spouse along with a cover sheet titled "Declaration of Disclosure" (FL-140). You must subsequently file a document titled, "Declaration Regarding Service of Declaration Disclosure and Income and Expense Declaration" (FL-141) with the court.

Step 10:

Once you have negotiated all relevant aspects of your divorce, your attorney or mediator will draft a Marital Separation Agreement ("MSA") or an attachment to a stipulated judgment (the effect of the two documents is the same). The MSA is filed alongside a Declaration for Default or Uncontested Dissolution or Legal Separation (FL-170). In addition, you must file a Judgment (FL-180) and a Notice of Entry of Judgment (FL-190). If all goes well, you will be divorced six months from the day your spouse is served with the summons.

CHAPTER 4

Division of Assets and Debts

"Splitting the financial pie"

California is a community property state, and the basic principle that governs the division of assets upon divorce seems simple enough: each spouse is entitled to one-half of the property that was acquired during the course of the marriage. As straightforward as this appears, the financial reality of dividing assets can be complex. Remember, upon divorce, you and your spouse are essentially selling everything you own to (a) each other, or (b) a third party.

Here are some of basic things you should know about asset division in California:

- Assets in California are classified in one of three categories: (1) community property, (2) quasi-community property, or (3) separate property.

- All property acquired during marriage and before separation, other than by gift or inheritance, is presumptively community property. California law calls for the equal division of community property upon divorce.

- All property acquired before marriage, after separation, or by gift or inheritance is separate property. Each spouse retains his or her own separate property upon divorce.

- Any debt incurred during the marriage is considered community property, regardless of who incurred it.

- If community property funds are used to pay down a separate property debt (i.e., a debt incurred by one spouse before marriage), the community is entitled to a reimbursement for the amount paid.

- When one spouse uses his or her separate property to acquire community property, he or she has a statutory "tracing right" of reimbursement. Such contributions include payments of principle (i.e., a down payment on a house), payments made to improve community property (i.e., an addition to a home), and payments that reduce the principal of a loan used to purchase or improve community property.

- A retirement account or plan is considered community property to the extent the benefit was earned during the course of the marriage.

- Some retirement plans are creatures of federal law, and as a result, they can only be divided by a special order, called a Qualified Domestic Relations Order (a "QDRO").

Asset Division, Practically Speaking

The intense stress of divorce often causes couples to ignore the many costs associated with dividing or selling assets. The consequences of doing so, however, can resonate for years to come. As with any other aspect of your divorce, you will benefit greatly if you and your spouse reach a fair settlement outside of court. Keep in mind that courts do not typically account for the many costs associated with maintaining and selling various assets, such as insurance, maintenance fees, commissions, and taxes. Nowhere is the disparity between the legal reality of divorce and the financial reality more glaring than when your assets are divided.

Consider the following simple scenario: John and Sue Smith are in the midst of a divorce. The Smiths have $100,000 in cash and shares of a mutual fund valued at $100,000. Despite the poor state of the economy, the mutual fund has done quite well, returning nearly 8% per year. Clearly the mutual fund has done much better than the tiny return earned by cash in a savings account. Therefore, it might seem that if the cash goes to John and the mutual fund to Sue, Sue is in a good position. After all, why not stick with a winning investment?

In reality, Sue is getting a raw deal. All of the accumulated capital gain will be taxed when the mutual fund is sold, and Sue will be wholly responsible for paying the taxes. If the Smiths held the shares for many years and saw the value rise significantly, the tax bill could be substantial—many thousands of dollars. The net effect is this: John is getting a better deal by walking away with cash.

Putting Together the Financial Puzzle

Transparency is the key to a quick and fair settlement. Both spouses must have a complete picture of the family finances before any meaningful discussion about the division of assets can occur. Cooperation will ultimately save both spouses an immense amount of money in legal fees. Discovery, the process used to request and disclose financial information, is exceedingly expensive and time consuming. Couples in high conflict divorces can easily find that discovery alone drastically reduces their net worth.

In many relationships, one spouse plays the role of financial planner. This spouse has a great advantage when it comes to obtaining a clear picture of the family finances. He or she may be tempted to "spin" the presentation of assets and liabilities to his or her advantage. This is particularly problematic in two situations: (1) when a privately held business represents a significant source of income, and (2) when one spouse operates a professional practice (medicine, law, accounting, etc.).

So how do you piece together the financial puzzle if you aren't the spouse who kept the books? First, try not to let the process overwhelm you. Many people find that getting a handle on the family finances is easier than they suspected it would be, largely because their spouse wrapped everything they did in a shroud of mystique. Some controlling spouses want to maintain the illusion that what they are doing is extremely complex. In most cases, the situation is not so mind-boggling. It may be a relief to know that no advanced math skills are required to piece everything together.

Do not wait until your divorce is well underway before beginning your financial investigation. Start immediately. If you are lucky and the family finances are nicely captured in a tidy set of books and records, the process should be relatively straightforward. If, like many couples, you and your spouse kept several boxes of receipts stashed around the house, getting an overview of your finances may take a bit more work. Here are basic places to start looking:

Tax returns: Assuming your spouse isn't a tax fraud (in which case you have bigger problems), your federal tax returns are an excellent starting point. If you don't have your tax returns for the past five years, you can obtain them from the IRS by filling out Form 4506. It's simple to download the form directly from the IRS website: www.irs.gov.

A careful analysis of a return can illuminate income that comes from a source other than W-2 wages. During this process, a previously overlooked asset may surface. When examining an income tax return, pay particular attention to the following schedules:

Schedule A – Itemized Deductions: Examine this schedule for real estate taxes and mortgage interest paid. The existence of such payments indicates the existence of real estate holdings, whether it's the family residence, a vacation home, or investment properties.

Schedule B – Interest and Ordinary Dividends: Income reflected on this schedule naturally indicates the existence of an underlying asset, which may be held in a brokerage or savings account. The amount of interest earned should give you some indication of the asset's value. Keep in mind, however, that many securities do not pay dividends. As a result, the existence of non-dividend-paying stock can't be ascertained by examining Schedule B.

Schedule C – Profit or Loss From Business: Be warned, business accounting is a complex discipline and is vulnerable to extensive manipulation. Couples who act like grownups and fully disclose all financial information won't play any of the income-hiding games that can plague the divorce process. Nevertheless, even well-meaning spouses can have an extremely hard time valuing a business. Analyzing the income from a business reported on Schedule C is a start, but it often only represents the tip of the iceberg. Understanding the accounting method a business uses is critical to understanding how a business reports income. Under the cash basis method, a business only reports cash income actually received, not money that is owed to it by customers. Expenses are deducted only if actually paid. Under the accrual basis method, income is reported when earned, not when it is actually received. Similarly, expenses are deducted when they are incurred, not when they are actually paid.

Schedule D – Capital Gains and Losses: This schedule reflects the sale or exchange of a capital asset. Virtually everything you own is a capital asset. When you sell the asset, any gain is taxed at capital gains rates.

Schedule E – Real Estate, Royalties, Partnerships, Trusts: This schedule will provide further evidence of rent-producing real estate. In addition, K-1 income from partnerships, S corporations, and limited liability companies will show up on Schedule E. If you become aware of the existence of any such entity, be sure to request a copy of the tax return for that organization. With regard to real estate, in particular, holding assets in a limited liability company is increasingly common. A limited liability company offers its members protection from liability while allowing so-called "flow through" taxation.

Bank and brokerage account statements: This may seem obvious, but obtaining these valuable statements can provide you with a wealth of financial information. A credit report (see below) should divulge the existence of most accounts.

Credit reports: Obtaining a credit report is easy. The Fair and Accurate Credit Transactions Act (FACTA) provides that the three major credit-reporting bureaus (Equifax, Experian, and TransUnion) must provide a free copy of your credit report every 12-month period. Simply call 1-877-322-8228, or visit www.annualcreditreport.com.

Title reports: Paying a visit to the county recorder's office and conducting a title search is a good way to determine if any liens have been placed on your real property (e.g., your home). If you would prefer not to manage this process yourself, the web is crowded with service providers who will happily conduct a title search for you.

Retirement plans: Be sure to keep tabs on any work-related pensions or savings accounts. Like everything else wholly or partly earned during the marriage, some or all of the value of these plans is community property.

Insurance policies: If you maintain a whole life policy, know the cash value of the policy. Regardless of whether the policy is whole life or term, be sure you keep track of who is listed as a beneficiary.

Credit and loan applications: These applications can be a good source of financial information.

Some assets are hard to miss. Your house, car, stocks and bonds, and retirement plans are relatively easy to track—and tough to forget. However, don't let other less significant assets slip away. Taken separately, they may not represent a large sum of money, but added together, they can make a difference. Such assets can include the following:

Vacation pay: Accumulated days of vacation should be valued based on the pay rate of the spouse who accrued the time off. In addition, some employers will compensate employees for unused sick days at the end of the year. This benefit can also be calculated and split.

Tickets to sporting or cultural events: For some couples, deciding what to do with a pair of highly-sought-after season tickets becomes quite contentious. Though the psychological value of the seats may be sky-high, valuing the tickets for divorce purposes isn't difficult. Many online resources exist that will give you a sense of what a third party might pay for the tickets.

Tax refunds: If you expect a tax refund, determining how it will be split is an important issue that should be addressed in your marital separation agreement.

Frequent flyer points: Valuing frequent flier points can be quite difficult. Some divorce professionals simply assign a monetary value to each point accumulated—two cents, for instance. Others recommend that the miles themselves be divided, or that one spouse issue a free ticket in the name of the other spouse. This is complicated by the fact that some airlines don't allow miles to be divided. A good starting point is simply reading the fine print on your frequent flier miles statement.

Club memberships: Country club or social club memberships are often quite valuable. In some cases, a club will require a significant up-front cash payment before granting membership. This sunk cost is something that should be accounted for in a divorce. In some instances, a couple is able to sell their membership interest and split the proceeds. In other cases, one spouse cashes out the other spouse by compensating him or her for half of the value of the membership.

Timeshares: Often a poor investment, a timeshare is sometimes worth less than the amount owed on it. If you and your spouse get along well, you may continue to own it jointly. If it's worth something, you may be able to sell it. If it's worth less than you owe, you may simply let it go into foreclosure.

A note about gifts: As a general rule, gifts received during marriage are the separate property of the spouse who obtained the gift. Sadly, gifts can create quite a bit of conflict in a divorce. If you are a husband who made a habit of giving your wife expensive jewelry, it's time to swallow hard and move on. The jewelry belongs to your wife and won't be split upon divorce. Likewise, if you are a generous wife who gave your husband an expensive piece of artwork for each birthday, you will likewise have to say goodbye to these valuable gifts.

Tracing gifts by family members is much more challenging. For instance, consider the following scenario: John Smith's father gave him $50,000 to buy a used sailboat. At that time, John was married to Sue. John took title to the property to the sailboat in his own name as his sole and separate property. John subsequently used community property funds to maintain the boat. Because the boat was bought with funds given to John by his father as a gift, it will be classified as John's separate property. However, Sue may be eligible for partial reimbursement for the maintenance done on the boat.

Hiding Assets

As always, spouses who freely share information reap incredible benefits in the long run—both financially and emotionally. Unfortunately, occasionally one spouse tries to hide assets from the other in contentious divorces. The logic is simple: if the other spouse is unaware of the existence of the asset, it won't be included in the pool of community property that must be divided. Aside from being highly unethical, this strategy can backfire horribly.

A favorite example that illustrates the foolishness of hiding assets is a well-known California case involving a woman who won a lottery jackpot of $1.3 million. Eleven days after winning the jackpot she decided she wanted to leave her husband of 25 years and filed for divorce. Of course, she never told her husband about the winnings, and she worked hard to keep the funds secret during the divorce proceedings. She was successful at first, but two years later the husband learned of her winnings when he received a misdirected piece of mail. A Superior Court judge was not amused by the wife's deception and, in accordance with the applicable law, ordered that the entire jackpot be given to the husband. The wife subsequently filed for bankruptcy.

Deceitful spouses have cooked up any number of schemes intended to hide assets from their spouse and save them money in a divorce. There is no end to the creativity attributable to these misguided spouses. If you suspect your spouse is performing financial gymnastics in an attempt to hide assets from you, you may need to hire a forensic accountant. It will cost you quite a bit of money, but a good forensic accountant can uncover any number of tricks. Here are a few examples of how a spouse might try to hide assets:

Paying money from a business to a close friend or family member, ostensibly for "services provided." In many cases, no work was ever done. The maneuver is simply a way to hide funds during the divorce process. As soon as the divorce is final, the friend or family member will invariably give the money back to the spouse.

Colluding with an employer to delay payment until after a divorce is final. This delayed payment might consist of a cash bonus, stock options, or simply deferred compensation. Uncovering this type of collusion is tricky, and often requires the use of a forensic accountant.

A few other common methods of hiding assets or income:

- Transferring money to a custodial account set up in the name of a child.

- Repaying a false debt to a friend.

- Attributing the purchase of luxurious goods (paintings, antique furniture, etc.) to business expenses.

- Delaying the consummation of an important business deal until after the divorce is final. This is considered hiding assets if it is done solely to lower the value of a business.

- Keeping cash in the form of traveler's checks or money orders.

Dividing the Investment Portfolio

If you have a financial advisor, consulting with him or her will be an important part of the divorce process. Some assets are subject to a number of complications such as confusing taxation or illiquidity. That said, if your financial situation isn't particularly complex, you should be able to split your investment portfolio without enlisting an army of advisors.

Determining which investment best serves your needs requires careful analysis. Just because owning a specific asset made perfect sense during the marriage doesn't mean that it makes any sense upon divorce. Remember that running two households is significantly more expensive than one. A high-risk, high-reward investment may no longer suit your needs.

When deciding how to apportion your portfolio, keep in mind your own appetite for managing various types of investments. Some investments, like rental properties and high-risk stocks, require a certain degree of vigilance to manage properly. Others, such as mutual funds and government bonds, require virtually no work at all. Consider both your appetite for risk and your ability to devote time to managing investments when divvying up your assets.

One simple maxim can help guide you through the mess of a divorce: "Sell it now." While selling an asset isn't the best course of action in every instance, in the vast majority of cases, disposing of assets before a divorce greatly simplifies the process. Selling the asset before the divorce allows you to share the selling costs and potential tax burden with your spouse.

Getting into the mindset of selling assets before the divorce will help you consider all the tax and other costs associated with the sale. This prevents confusion regarding the true net value of an asset. To make wise decisions during the asset division process, it is essential that you understand the concept of tax basis. For a purchased investment, the tax basis is the amount paid. If inherited, the tax basis is the value of the asset on the date of the original owner's death. If received as a gift, the tax basis is the amount that was originally paid for the investment, unless the market value of the investment on the date the gift was given was lower.

Capital gain is determined by subtracting the tax basis of the asset from the sale price. No one likes to take a loss, but remember that selling an asset and taking a loss is the ideal way to offset a gain. Consider the following example:

Sue and John buy shares of Company X stock for a total of $4,000 and shares of Company Z stock for a total of $4,000. Two years later, they sell the Company X stock for $2,000, taking a $2,000 loss. Two weeks later, they sell the Company Z stock for $6,500, taking a $2,500 gain. If they didn't sell the Company X stock, their capital gains tax would be $375. However, due to the loss offset resulting from the sale of the Company X stock, their capital gains tax is only $75 ($2,500 gain minus $2,000 loss multiplied by 15%).

This simply goes to show that thinking strategically when liquidating assets during the divorce process can save you money. The stress of divorce can cause spouses to shut down a part of the mind that is more critical than ever—the ability to think strategically when it comes to their finances.

Valuing Assets

For those divorcing couples who are committed to doing things the grownup way—coming to a fair agreement outside of court—determining the value of each asset ranges from incredibly simple to fairly complex. The following information should help you get started:

Cash and receivables: Simply perusing your bank account statements should give you an accurate picture of the amount of cash you hold. Don't forget to search your files for copies of any receivables (i.e., money due to you under a personal loan). Sometimes families lend money to other relatives on an informal basis. While formalizing such loans is essential and avoids the inference that such a loan was actually a gift, many individuals skip this important step. As a result, you should try to locate evidence of all loans (informal and formal) you or your spouse have made to other individuals.

Stocks and bonds: If you use a brokerage firm or an online service to purchase your stocks, you can either (i) call the firm's trading department and ask them to give you the current price of a stock or fund, (ii) simply check the business section of the paper, or (iii) locate the price on any one of the numerous financial websites that crowd the Internet. Your brokerage firm should be able to help you with the value of your bonds.

Insurance: Assuming you are listed as the owner of the policy, the insurance company or broker who obtained the policy for you should be able to give you the policy's current value and surrender value. If you don't own the policy and you have a cooperative spouse, ask your spouse to provide you with the required information. If you are embroiled in litigation, this information may simply come out during the discovery process.

Collectibles and other personal property: A highly-regarded estate planning attorney once remarked, "The second you walk out the shop door with a piece of jewelry or a collectible, you've taken a 50% loss." There is a great deal of truth to his off-the-cuff comment. Collectibles are rarely worth as much as their owners like to believe. The key here is to get an appraisal. When valuing an item, make sure you use its resale value, not its retail price.

Unfortunately, you may hear a host of different values according to who is performing the appraisal. The trick is to find a valuation that both you and your spouse find acceptable.

The closely-held business: Because they aren't listed on the various exchanges and therefore aren't readily liquid, partnership interests, stock in privately held corporations, and membership interests in a limited liability company can be quite difficult to value.

Appraising a private business is part art, part science. In a contested divorce, valuing a small business can turn into a battle of the appraisers. Thankfully, though, valuing a company is less of a guessing game than it used to be, partially due to a constantly growing database of information on comparable sales, which can be accessed through entities such as BizComps and the Institute of Business Appraisers.

While a public company can fetch upward of thirty times its earnings on the market, a private company may be lucky to sell for five times its annual earnings. Buyers place a premium on one simple factor: predictable and growing cash flow. Of course, if you're dealing with promising intellectual property in its infancy, the cash flow analysis is less important. A company with attractive intellectual property may sell for many times its annual earnings. Indeed, a company with no earnings may still be quite valuable if it holds a patent that is well positioned to influence a particular marketplace in the future.

Certain intangibles also affect the value of a business. Location can be very important. A technology company in San Jose might garner a higher bid than a rival in Stockton simply because of the quality of the workforce and its proximity to the industry's nexus. Likewise, a company that manufactures a car part with ten customers will fetch a lower price than a competitor of similar size that boasts fifty reliable customers because it doesn't enjoy a revenue source that is quite as diversified.

A private company that is on the cusp of going public will undoubtedly fetch a much higher price than one that is less growth oriented. And a company that is likely to be sold to a "strategic buyer" (one that will use the company to expand its product line or territory) will garner a generous price.

Sound complicated? It certainly can be. If you own a "mom and pop" store that has maintained fairly consistent revenue over the course of two decades, valuation should be relatively simple. If you own a company that is growing quickly, or that has developed some particularly valuable intellectual property, you will need a great deal of help. Professional assistance can come at quite a cost, but it is the only way to get a reasonable ballpark figure.

Selecting the right professional to appraise your business can be equally daunting. A CPA with no specialized training in business valuation is probably a poor choice, while one who is a certified valuation analyst is a better bet. A mergers and acquisitions specialist may also be able to provide you with a reasonable appraisal.

Keep in mind that appraising your business can involve quite a bit of work on your part. Already emotionally exhausted from your divorce, the last thing you'll want to do is gear up for a tedious valuation. You can expect to produce several years of financial statements and explain them in excruciating detail.

How much does a business appraisal cost? It varies according to the size of your company, but to give you a general sense of the fees involved: a business with less than $1 million in annual sales and good record keeping might incur a fee of $5,000. A company with $15 million in sales could pay many times that amount simply due to the complexity of its accounts.

Stock options: An increasingly important part of many employees' compensation packages, stock options require careful consideration during the divorce process. Stock options are deceivingly simple compensation contracts. When an option is exercised, its payoff rises by one dollar for each dollar the stock price is above the exercise price (also called the "strike price"). If the stock price is below the exercise price when the option matures, the option is not exercised and it has zero payoff. Despite the basic nature of this concept, few employees truly grasp all of the implications of option ownership. Indeed, surveys have shown that employees tend to place unrealistic expectations on their options and hold them in higher esteem than their value merits.

The complexity of dividing options upon divorce depends on whether the options have vested or not. If a spouse's stock options have vested during the course of the marriage, the options are clearly community property and are therefore subject to equal division. However, the situation gets more complicated when some or all of the options haven't yet vested.

California courts acknowledge that unvested options, though they have no present value, are subject to division. The manner in which a court determines what portion of the unvested options belongs to each spouse varies from case to case, and a judge has wide discretion in deciding which formula or approach to use in allocating options. In general, the longer the interval between separation and the date the options vest, the smaller the portion allocated to the non-employee spouse will be. For example, if a significant number of options vest only a few months after separation, a large portion of those shares will be considered community property. However, if a significant number of options vest three years after the date of separation, a much smaller portion will be considered community property.

In most cases, a court will use one of two formulas when determining how many options should be considered community property. Before applying one of the formulas, though, a court often determines whether the options were granted to the employee as a reward for past services, to attract the employee to the job in the first place, or as an incentive to stay with the company in anticipation of future job performance.

If the court determines that the options were granted to the employee spouse (1) as a reward for past service, or (2) as an upfront incentive to attract the employee to the job, the following formula may apply:

Community Property Shares =   [(DOH—DOS) / (DOH –DOE)] x [Shares Exercisable]
where "DOH" = Date of Hire
and "DOS" = Date of Separation
and "DOE" = Date of Options May be Exercised

To illustrate how this might work, let's use the example of John and Sue Smith. John and Sue live in Silicon Valley. John started working at a start-up company, TechComp, on January 1, 2010. After three years at TechComp, the CEO expressed his delight at John's performance by offering him 1,000 options, exercisable on a four-year vesting schedule. In other words, 250 of John's options were scheduled to vest each year. For three years John exercised his options in accordance with his option agreement. Because 750 shares of TechComp vested during his marriage to Sue, all 750 shares are clearly considered community property. However, on August 2, 2016, 152 days before John earned the ability to exercise the last 250 options, he and Sue separated.

Applying the formula set forth above to the last 250 options, then, we have:

Community Property Shares =
[(DOH—DOS) / (DOH –DOE)] x Shares Exercisable

Community Property Shares =
[(2405 days) / (2557 days)] x 250 Shares

Community Property Shares = <u>235</u> Shares

Note that the vast majority of the shares that vest on January 1, 2017 are considered community property. This makes sense, as the reason behind granting the options (rewarding John for past performance) hinged upon his performance during the marriage.

Contrast the above formula with the approach that is used when options are granted as an incentive to keep an employee with a company:

Community Property Shares =   [(DOG—DOS) / (DOG –DOE)] x [shares exercisable]
where "DOG" = Date of Grant
and "DOS" = Date of Separation
and "DOE" = Date of Options May be Exercised

To illustrate how this formula works, and how it generates a different result, let's alter the facts in the example set forth above. This time, on January 1, 2013, after John has worked for three years with TechComp, the CEO becomes worried that John may leave, and as an incentive to keep him around, he offers John 1,000 options, vesting on the same four-year schedule.

Applying the formula set forth above, we have:

Community Property Shares =
[(DOG—DOS) / (DOG –DOE)] x Shares Exercisable

Community Property Shares =
[(1309 days) / (1461 days)] x 250 Shares

Community Property Shares = <u>223</u> Shares

Clearly the two methods offer different results when it comes to calculating the number of options that should be considered community property. In the end, if you decide to litigate your divorce, the judge will decide which method he or she prefers (or indeed, use another method entirely). If you and your spouse mediate your divorce, the two formulas can provide a reasonable backdrop for your discussions.

Of course, the analysis set forth above is only the tip of the iceberg when it comes to stock options. Stock options and other equity incentive devices come in many formats. Two commonly seen iterations include incentive stock options (ISOs) and nonqualified stock options (NQSOs).

ISOs can only be granted to employees of the underlying company and benefit from favorable tax treatment. Upon exercise of ISOs, the employee does not have to pay ordinary income tax on the difference between the exercise price and the fair market value of the shares issued. Rather, if the shares are held long enough (one year from the date of exercise and two years from the date of the option grant), the profit from the sale of the shares is taxed at the long-term capital gains rate.

NQSOs don't qualify for the special treatment granted to incentive stock options. Instead of being taxed at the long-term capital gain rate, NQSOs are taxed as income to the recipient at the time of exercise. As you might expect, this less favorable tax treatment comes with far fewer restrictions with regard to the timing of exercise.

Regardless of the nature of the equity incentives you or your spouse have earned, you should consider enlisting the help of an accountant or other executive compensation specialist in determining how the taxation of your incentives will affect their value. The IRS rules regarding the taxation of stock options transferred between spouses upon divorce are complex, and you will most certainly appreciate the help.

Spouses frequently "trade" options for other property when negotiating a divorce settlement. A spouse who has labored away at a start-up company may feel strongly about retaining all of his or her options, though this insistence on retaining all the options is typically misguided. To many employees, stock options represent a chance, however miniscule, at striking it rich—a dream that doesn't typically accompany a "boring" standard salary. Before trading the right to options for other property, it is important to get a firm grasp on the value of the options. Various models of valuing options exist, and when dealing with early-stage startup companies, the process is more art than science. As with deciphering the tax implications of transferring options upon divorce, enlisting expert help when valuing options will greatly ease the strain of the divorce process.

Retirement Benefits

For many couples, a pension or retirement account is not only a sizeable asset, but it also an asset that may carry significant personal value to one spouse. Like virtually everything else, a retirement account is considered community property to the extent the benefit was earned during the course of the marriage. Dividing a retirement plan is no small task, and the vehicle used to effectively split a plan varies according to the type of plan.

First, understand that most retirement plans broadly fall into two categories: (1) defined benefit plans, and (2) defined contribution plans. Defined benefit plans are often called pension plans, and in such a plan, an employer often pays the employee a monthly sum until the employee dies. Defined contribution plans, on the other hand, usually constitute a mixture of contributions by both the employee and the employer. A 401(k) plan is an easy example of a defined contribution plan. An Individual Retirement Account (IRA), while a close cousin of the defined contribution plan, stands on its own.

Valuing a defined benefit plan can be difficult simply because doing so involves actuarial calculations. In other words, the value of the plan depends on several variables, including the rate of inflation and the life expectancy of the beneficiaries. Dividing such a plan is therefore correspondingly complex. A defined contribution plan or an IRA is much simpler to value, simply because the plan administrator will report the current value of the account to the holder in regular statements.

What portion of a plan is community property? A simple calculation is typically used to determine how much of a retirement plan will be considered community property (this is often referred to as the "California Time Rule":

1) First, determine the total number of months of plan participation.

2) Next, determine the number of months of plan participation between the date of marriage and the date of separation.

3) Finally, divide the first number by the second to obtain the percentage ownership interest.

Consider this example:

John Smith works for a manufacturing company that offers a generous defined benefit plan (a pension). He has been accruing retirement under the plan for 23 years (276 months), and has been married to Sue for 19.5 of those years (234 months). The percentage of the pension that is community property is therefore 85% (234 divided by 276). Sue is therefore entitled to ½ of the community property share (or 42.5%), while John is entitled to both ½ of the community share and his separate property share (a total of 57.5%).

The valuation method has a drawback, of course, and that is the simple fact that the contributions to the plan early in employment (typically when an employee's salary is lower) are less valuable than the contributions made later in employment (when an employee's salary is higher). A precise calculation may require the help of an actuary, pension administrator, or financial planner.

Sometimes spouses are shocked when presented with the actual present value of a seemingly sizeable plan. We all know that a dollar today is worth far more than a dollar ten years from now.

Nevertheless, the degree to which the "present value factor" can diminish the current value of the plan is often startling. Here's an example using simplified data:

Tim Larsen is 42 years old. Upon retirement at age 65, his plan will pay him $20,000 annually for the rest of his life. Let's assume actuarial tables state that Tim should live until age 75. Theoretically, then, he should receive a total of $200,000 ($20,000 per year multiplied by 10 years). Remember, of course, that Tim won't retire for another 23 years. Assuming a 4% inflation rate, the present value of Tim's right to receive $20,000 for 10 years starting at age 65 is roughly $50,000. His wife, Tina Larsen, is therefore surprised to learn that her 42.5% share in the plan is only worth approximately $21,000. If she waits until Tim retires, she will be eligible to receive a much larger sum. Such is the nature of present value calculations.

Present value calculations can be done using present value tables or, even better, an online calculator. Many reputable websites offer free present value calculators that are quite simple to use (www.investopedia.com is one example).

The mechanics of retirement plan division: Dividing different types of plans requires different types of orders. Retirement plans that are controlled by federal law (which preempts state law) must be divided by an order known as a Qualified Domestic Relations Order (a" QDRO"—pronounced "quadro"). Other plans can be divided by a state court order alone. A QDRO is an extremely important document, and it must be perfectly accurate, simply because anything omitted from the order can't be reinstated later. Virtually all mediators, and most family lawyers, rely on specialists to draft QDROs.

The following table sets forth a few of the common types of plans and the type of order required.

Plan Type	Type of Order Required to Divide Plan
401(K)	QDRO
Thrift Savings Plan	QDRO
Employee Stock Ownership Plan (ESOP)	QDRO
Tax Sheltered Annuities (TSAs)	QDRO
Traditional IRA	Ordinary court order
Roth IRA	Ordinary court order
Deferred Annuity	Ordinary court order
Corporate or Business Pension	QDRO
Military Pension	Subject to very specific government regulations regarding division upon divorce

Income tax considerations associated with retirement accounts: The IRS always gets its share. True, some retirement plans have very real tax advantages, but the IRS always takes a bite of the money you accrue for retirement at some point.

A common trade-off used by divorcing couples allows one spouse to take the retirement plan while the other retains the equity in the family home. If you are the spouse taking the retirement plan, you need to understand how withdrawals from the plan will be taxed to determine if it is a fair trade. Ideally, the retirement plan was funded with after-tax dollars, which means that you will be able to withdraw part of the proceeds at retirement without being taxed.

By either contacting the retirement plan administrator or checking your annual benefits statement, you should be able to determine the ratio of pre-tax to after-tax contributions. As a general rule, if your employer partly funded a retirement plan (i.e., with matching contributions in a 401(k), for instance) the portion that the employer contributed will be taxed when withdrawn at retirement.

Keep in mind that you do not pay taxes on money that you contribute to a traditional IRA. However, a Roth IRA works very differently. You are taxed on the money you contribute to a Roth IRA at the time of contribution, but you receive the benefits tax-free upon retirement. This clearly makes receiving a Roth IRA a more attractive proposition upon divorce.

The true value of an account: The date of separation is critically important when valuing a retirement plan. As is the case with the income of either spouse, any increase in the value of the plan after the date of separation is the separate property of the beneficiary spouse. Contrast this with the way in which assets are valued—at the date of trial. This may lead to confusion, even among financial professionals. Consider the following example:

John and Sue Smith decide to divorce in 2008. John moves out of the house and rents an apartment. Neither John nor Sue hopes for reconciliation. However, John and Sue aren't in any great hurry to get divorced, and they don't complete the process until 2012. All of the appreciation in John's retirement plan between 2008 and 2012 is considered his separate property. Sue is therefore only entitled to half of the value of his retirement plan as valued from the date of their marriage to the date of separation.

Calculating the true value of a retirement plan is an important part of the asset division process. It can seem daunting at first, and some people choose to have a third party (such as an accountant) value a retirement plan.

Division of Debt

For many married couples, dividing debt is just as important as dividing assets. Again, remember that any debt incurred during marriage and prior to separation is community property, regardless of who incurred it. This means that if your spouse secretly racked up massive credit card debt while you were married, you are out of luck. However, this is a glimmer of hope, and that involves the nature of the debt. If the debt was incurred to benefit the "community," i.e., the two of you, it is considered community property. However, if the debt was incurred solely for the benefit of one spouse, relief *may* be available. Consider the following example:

Anthony and Maria Andretti live modestly. They make timely payments on their mortgage, take a single inexpensive family vacation per year, and rarely eat at nice restaurants. Anthony completely manages the family finances, from balancing the checkbook to paying credit card bills. Unbeknownst to Maria, while they were living in the same house (and separation wasn't yet being discussed), Anthony was incurring huge credit card bills on hotel rooms and lavish meals in an attempt to impress his young lover. Maria is greatly relieved to learn that the debt associated with Anthony's seduction of his lover is his separate property.

Note, however, that Maria's relief may be short lived. While a court can certainly divide debt and order that one spouse is solely responsible for a particular debt, credit card companies are not hindered by these orders if the credit card was a joint card. Creditors may still collect from either spouse. The only remedy for the aggrieved spouse is to go after the spouse who incurred the debt for reimbursement.

Use of community property to pay pre-marital debt: Sometimes one spouse enters a marriage with debt. If community property funds are used to pay down that separate property debt, the community is entitled to a reimbursement for the amount it paid. Consider the following example:

Sue Smith had large credit card debts incurred prior to marrying John. To improve their credit rating so they could buy a house, Sue and John worked hard to pay off the debt using community property funds. Now that they are debt free, Sue files for divorce. Because Sue and John used community property earnings to pay off Sue's separate property debt, the community is entitled to reimbursement for the amount paid. In other words, John should ultimately recover half of the amount used to pay off Sue's debt, as half of all community property is his.

Use of separate property to pay community property debt: In California, if one spouse's separate property is used to pay off a community property debt, a court will presume that a gift was made to the community. However, there is an important exception to this rule. When one spouse uses his or her separate property to acquire community property, he or she has a statutory "tracing right" of reimbursement. Such contributions include payments of principal (i.e., a down payment on a house), payments made to improve community property (i.e., an addition to a home), and payments that reduce the principal of a loan used to purchase or improve community property. Note that this does not include payments for maintenance of the property, interest on the underlying loan, or taxation. Consider the following examples:

Example 1: Carrie and Marcus Olefsky decide to send their child, Bobby, to private school. Marcus uses funds from his separate property brokerage account to pay the tuition. He is not entitled to reimbursement from the community for this payment. It is considered a gift to the community.

Example 2: Luis and Rosa Lopez want to purchase a home. Luis has significant savings that he accumulated prior to marriage. He uses these savings to make the down payment on their new home. Luis is entitled to "trace" this contribution back to his separate property, meaning he has a right of reimbursement from the community for the amount of the down payment.

Example 3: Seo and Mingi Tran decide their home is too small, and Seo uses savings that he accumulated prior to marriage to "improve" the property by adding an extra room. Seo is entitled to trace this contribution back to his separate property, and he is therefore entitled to reimbursement from the community.

Example 4: Jake and Elizabeth Williams are struggling to pay all of the expenses associated with living in their home. As a result, Jake agrees to pay for the maintenance of the home and all associated property taxes using his separate property savings. Unfortunately for Jake, he is not entitled to reimbursement from the community for any of this amount. Had Jake used his separate property to make principal payments on the mortgage, he could trace his contribution and qualify for reimbursement. However, because Jake used his funds to pay taxes and maintenance costs associated with the home, he is out of luck.

Use of separate property to pay community property debt after separation: Once a couple has separated, a spouse who uses separate property to pay pre-existing community debt is entitled to reimbursement from the community. This reverses the presumption of a gift that exists when separate property is used to pay a community debt before separation. Note, however, that there are a few exceptions to this rule. The first is that the paying spouse is entitled to reimbursement only *when the amount paid is substantially in excess of the value of the use*. This may sound like a mouthful, but all it means is that a spouse who enjoys the use of the property should not be reimbursed for paying down debt associated with that property, so long as the value of the use is roughly equal to the amount paid. Consider the following example:

John and Sue Smith separate, and John continues to make loan payments on his pickup truck. The loan is community property, but Sue never drives the truck—John is the only one who enjoys the benefit of the truck. As a result, the payments John makes on his pickup truck can be correlated to his use of the truck. He is therefore not entitled to reimbursement from the community for the loan payments, even if the truck is held jointly.

There are two additional exceptions to the rule that a spouse is entitled to reimbursement for amounts contributed to pay off a community debt after separation: (1) where the parties have agreed that the payments will not be reimbursed, and (2) where the payments were intended as a gift or as child support or spousal support.

Use of community property funds to pay separate living expenses after separation: The community is only entitled to reimbursement when one spouse uses community property funds to pay his or her separate living expenses to the extent that those expenses *exceed a reasonable amount of child support and spousal support*. Of course, as is the case in so many areas of the law, understanding the meaning of the term "reasonable" is important. While the term will vary from case to case, a reasonable amount would probably be the amount of guideline support that a court would order in an application for temporary child and spousal support. Consider the following example:

After separating from John Smith, Sue remains in the family home and continues to care for their son, Bobby. Sue's part-time work brings home only $1,500 a month, and as a result, let's assume a court would likely order that John pay her $3,000 per month in temporary child support and spousal support. However, Sue is waist-deep in a midlife crisis, and she soon finds herself spending $7,000 a month to support her new lifestyle. She sells $5,500 worth of stock from the Smith's community property stock portfolio each month for five months to make ends meet. A judge might order that Sue reimburse the community to the tune of $12,500 ($2,500 per month for five months). Remember, the community would likely be entitled to reimbursement only for the amount spent that exceeds guideline support. Here, Sue spent $5,500 in community property funds for five months, when guideline support would have totaled $3,000 per month.

One spouse remains in primary residence while other spouse makes mortgage payments: Quite often one spouse moves out of the family home during separation while the other spouse remains in the home. The spouse who leaves may offer to keep paying the mortgage and property taxes. Unless these payments are made in accordance with an agreement to waive reimbursement or the payments are a form of child or spousal support, the paying spouse may be entitled to reimbursement because he or she is paying a community debt with separate property funds.

Lastly, the spouse who stays in the home could be in trouble in a contested divorce if the fair market rental value of the home exceeds the mortgage payments. If a home was recently purchased, the mortgage payments will almost always exceed the fair market rental value of a home. However, this is often not the case with older properties. A home bought twenty years ago may be encumbered by a fairly modest mortgage. However, in the intervening twenty years, the fair market rental value of the home may have increased dramatically. The spouse remaining in the home after separation may therefore be required to reimburse the community for the difference between the mortgage payments and the fair market rental value of the home between the date of separation and the date of trial. Consider the following example:

John and Sue Smith decide to separate, and they both agree that Sue should stay in the home with their son, Bobby. John continues to pay the mortgage using the income from his job. The Smith's bought their home 20 years ago, and as a result, their mortgage payments are a modest $1,500 per month. However, the fair market rental value of their home is $2,500. The Smiths separated ten months before their divorce becomes final. As a result, Sue may owe the community $10,000 ($2,500 - $1,500 multiplied by 10). And it doesn't stop there. The community may also be entitled to reimbursement for the mortgage payments themselves (another $15,000). In the end, Sue will be dismayed to know that she owes a total of $25,000 to the community simply because she was allowed to remain in the home during the period of separation. The net cost to Sue is $12,500 (because half of the community is hers, after all), and the net benefit to John is $12,500 (because half of the community is his).

The lesson here? If you are the spouse remaining in the home during separation, make absolutely sure that you document in writing that the privilege of remaining in the house should be considered an element of spousal support (or child support, if applicable) and that the paying spouse should not receive any reimbursement as a result.

Bankruptcy and Divorce

It's a sad truth—for some couples, bankruptcy is simply a part of the divorce process. Indeed, financial woes are often the cause of the divorce itself. When debts become so overwhelming that a couple sees no way out, filing for bankruptcy may be the best option. Before coming to the decision to file bankruptcy, though, you should exhaust all other options. A bankruptcy will destroy your credit for many years to come and may affect your ability to rent an apartment, get a job, or qualify for a loan of any amount. Furthermore, declaring bankruptcy is much harder than it used to be, thanks in large part to the Bankruptcy Abuse Prevention and Consumer Protection Act of 2005.

First, it is important to understand the difference between the two most common types of bankruptcy: Chapter 7 and Chapter 13. Chapter 7 allows you to discharge all of your debts forever. Chapter 13, on the other hand, is a "reorganization" and requires that you pay some of your debt. The 2005 Act has made it much harder to qualify for the more forgiving Chapter 7 bankruptcy. For instance, if your income is above your state's median income, you have to file for Chapter 13 in all but the most extraordinary of circumstances. Even if your income is below the state median, you have to file for Chapter 13 if you can pay more than $100 per month on your unsecured debt over the following five years.

Various types of debt can't be discharged by bankruptcy, including student loans, judgments involving restitution for a crime, and debts obtained by fraud. In addition, the 2005 Act made the rules regarding the discharge of support-related debts even more stringent—it is now difficult, if not impossible, to get out of such payments through bankruptcy.

Pay close attention to your settlement agreement to make sure it doesn't leave you unprotected in the event that your former spouse declares bankruptcy. In some cases, one spouse has no assets to give to the other spouse in exchange for receiving the bulk of the community property (i.e., the family home). As a result, the spouse receiving the larger share of community property may give the other spouse a promissory note. First of all, consider securing the promissory note with a lien on the primary residence. Second, your promissory note receivable is much more likely to survive bankruptcy if you specify in the settlement agreement that the note is made in lieu of alimony.

Keep in mind that bankruptcy is a creature of federal, not state, law. As a result, filing for bankruptcy in the midst of a divorce can create a true mess. The family court is allowed to continue to decide issues regarding the establishment of spousal and child support, but it may not apportion investments, divide the family home, or distribute any other property until federal bankruptcy court grants its permission.

Most importantly, if you are considering filing for bankruptcy, seek the counsel of an experienced bankruptcy attorney. While a family law attorney is likely familiar with the basics of bankruptcy, you should consult with someone who substantially limits his or her practice to bankruptcy.

The Legal Framework for Asset Division

The legal framework surrounding asset division is set forth in California Family Code Sections 2550 through 2660 (Exhibit E of the Appendix).

Classification of Property

Before property can be divided and distributed, it must be characterized as "community property," "separate property," or "quasi-community property" as defined in the California Family Code.

Separate property: Any property acquired before marriage or after separation is considered the acquiring spouse's separate property. The time of acquisition is therefore important, and is typically set at the time when the original property right arose. For example, with regard to an automobile, the time of acquisition would be the date the purchase contract was signed, not the date the DMV confirmed title.

Property acquired by "gift, bequest, devise, or descent" is also characterized as separate property. For example, if your father leaves you $100,000 in his will, that money is your separate property. Likewise, if your spouse gives you a diamond necklace, the gift is your separate property.

In addition, any assets acquired after the date of separation (but before divorce) are considered the separate property of the acquiring spouse. For example, if your date of separation is June 15 and you buy a new automobile on September 15 using payments you received in the interim as temporary support, that automobile is your separate property.

Community property: All property acquired during the marriage and before separation, other than by gift or inheritance, is presumptively community property. This includes all compensation, regardless of the form it takes, a concept that will become more important when determining how much (if any) child support or spousal support is appropriate.

The following are examples of compensation:

- Stock in lieu of salary

- Employer contributions to an employee profit-sharing plan

- Incentive stock options

- A "gift" from an employer (of real estate, for instance), which is in reality deferred compensation in lieu of a pension

- Vacation pay, or the right to receive certain other financial benefits as deferred compensation upon termination of employment

All earnings from a privately held business are considered community property to the extent they reflect either spouse's participation in the business. On the other hand, earnings that don't reflect the labor or skill of either spouse are considered a return on a capital investment and are characterized as separate or community property based on the date of the original investment. This may sound confusing at first blush, but the concept is sensible. Consider the following example:

Before marrying Sue, John Smith invested in a fast food franchise along with two of his close friends. The franchise did fairly well, but by the time John and Sue were married, he was a completely silent partner. He did nothing more than collect his share of the profits generated by the franchise. The income generated by the franchise that is payable to John is his separate property. He performed no work to generate those profits during the course of his marriage to Sue. The "seed was sown" before they were married. Therefore the earnings from the franchise are not community property.

Contrast the previous example with the following: Before marrying Sue, John opened an accounting practice. Getting started took quite a bit of time, and the practice wasn't even profitable by the time he married Sue. In this case, valuing the business will be quite difficult. Some portion of goodwill is attributable to the work John did before marriage, but the income derived from the practice after marriage clearly reflects John's labor and skill, and is therefore community property. In a case like this, and outside expert may be required to properly value the business.

As a general rule, simply remember that any asset obtained or income earned during the marriage is community property. This includes the right to receive income in the future—for instance, through a grant of stock options, or perhaps through deferred compensation.

California Family Code Section 910 states that any debt incurred during the marriage and prior to separation is community property. It also doesn't matter whose name appears on a bill or a credit card statement. If it was incurred during the marriage and prior to separation, it's a community property debt and both spouses are equally liable. However, potential relief may be offered by Family Code Section 2625, which gives the court the power to assign a debt incurred during the marriage to one spouse if it was not "incurred for the benefit of the community."

Quasi-community property: California Family Code sections 125(a) and 125(b) define "Quasi-community property." In short, quasi-community property is real estate and personal property acquired by a spouse while living out of state that would have been community property if the spouse had been domiciled in California. The definition of quasi-community property also includes any property that is acquired in exchange for such property. Quasi-community property is a means for California courts to obtain the authority to dispose of non-California assets in a divorce.

Important Legal Concepts Applicable to Asset Division

The following legal concepts play an important role in the division of property upon divorce in California·

Assets v. income: Assets and income are treated very differently in divorce. Your community property *assets* are divided equally, while *income* is used to determine how much spousal support and child support is appropriate.

Date of separation: In dividing earnings and income, the date of separation becomes a very important factor. California Family Code Section 771 indicates that "separation" requires more than a rift in the spouses' relationship. The "date of separation" occurs only when the parties have parted ways with no present intent to resume their marriage. The conduct of the spouses must demonstrate a complete and final break in the marital relationship.

For example, Sue and John agree that their marriage is troubled. On August 1st they decide to separate to "test the waters." John moves out of the house. They both agree that they want to preserve the possibility of getting back together. December 5 rolls around, and John sends Sue a letter stating that the marriage is over, he isn't coming home, and he wants a divorce. The date of separation is December 5, not August 1. The decision to separate on August 1 is too tentative to reflect the "date of separation" under California law. Any earnings or assets accumulated between August 1 and December 5 are community property.

Date of divorce: Unlike earnings and income, which lose their community property nature after the date of separation, community property assets are valued as near as possible to the date of judgment. According to California Family Code Section 2552, "the court shall value the assets and liabilities as near as practicable to the time of trial." In other words, if a community property asset appreciates significantly during the interval between separation and divorce, that appreciation is split evenly between the parties.

Transmutation: As set forth in California Family Code Section 850(a)(b) and (c), spouses may agree to change the nature of any or all of their property. In other words, they can agree to change separate property into community property and vice versa. This may be accomplished by a marital property agreement. In addition, California courts will typically honor premarital agreements that are entered into freely and knowingly, and that alter each spouse's property rights as set forth by California law.

CHAPTER 5

Spousal Support

"The 'S' Words"

Commonly known as alimony, spousal support is a topic that often generates great conflict between couples. Most parents readily acknowledge that they have a moral duty to support their children, and their ability to do so may be a matter of pride. Supporting a former spouse, however, is a concept that often meets with strong resistance. While some individuals will acknowledge that their former spouse is entitled to payments for a certain period of time, most cringe at the thought of continuing to support their former spouse long after divorce.

Here are some of basic things you should know about spousal support in California:

- Marriages broadly fall into two categories: marriages of long duration (over 10 years) and marriages of short duration (under 10 years).

- For a marriage of short duration, spousal support payments typically continue for one-half the length of the marriage (i.e., 3 years for a 6-year marriage).

- For a marriage of long duration, spousal support may be indefinite, but a court may also order a conditional termination date (i.e., payments terminate after 10 years unless the receiving spouse successfully petitions the court to extend payments).

- Temporary spousal support is usually a larger figure than permanent spousal support.

- Temporary spousal support is typically set by reference to a schedule based on income.

- Permanent spousal support is based on a court's analysis of several different factors, including the income of each spouse, living expenses, the standard of living enjoyed by the couple during the marriage, and the future earning capacity of each spouse.

- Spousal support may not be modified solely due to an increase in the paying spouse's income.

- Spousal support may be modified upward if the receiving spouse demonstrates a reduction in income or an increase in expenses.

- Spousal support may be modified downward if the receiving spouse cohabitates with an individual of the opposite sex.

- Unless otherwise agreed upon by the parties, spousal support terminates when the receiving party remarries.

- Spousal support is treated as taxable income to the receiving spouse and may be deducted from income (for income tax purposes) by the paying spouse.

Spousal Support, Practically Speaking

The notion that spousal support will allow each spouse to enjoy the standard of living he or she experienced while married is misplaced. Simply put, providing for two households is more expensive than providing for one. Instead of a single rent or mortgage payment, you may end up with two. You may lose the economy of scale associated with feeding more than one person. If you enjoyed health coverage through your spouse's employer, another policy will have to be purchased. Family-rate memberships will have to be terminated and restructured as individual memberships. If you have children and your spouse gets the practical car, leaving you with the two-seater, you may need to buy a new kid-friendly car.

All told, your standard of living is likely to decrease at least slightly when you divorce. There are a few exceptions to this rule. Strangely enough, the IRS does incentivize divorce when one spouse brings home nearly all of the household income by offering the couple an enormous tax break—the deductibility of spousal support. In situations involving the division of one spouse's income between two individuals through spousal support, the cost of maintaining two households is mitigated. Likewise, if one spouse moves to a much cheaper part of the state, that spouse may be able to enjoy a higher standard of living on less income. In most cases, though, it is naïve to think that both spouses can enjoy a standard of living similar to that which they enjoyed while married.

Generally speaking, the goal of spousal support is to grant the lower-income spouse enough time to become self-sufficient. This doesn't mean that the lower-income spouse must succeed in attaining the same salary as the higher-earning spouse. Instead, spousal support merely offers the lower income spouse the opportunity to lay the foundation for a life that is comfortable and sustainable. This might entail earning a degree, obtaining a certification, or simply learning a new trade.

In marriages of extremely long duration involving one spouse who hasn't worked for years, lifetime support is sometimes awarded. This is simply because one spouse has been a homemaker for so long that expecting that spouse to go out and find a job is unreasonable. In most cases, however, spousal support will only continue for a period of months or years.

Every marriage is different, every family has unique needs, and no single formula will magically generate the ideal spousal support figure. Unlike child support calculations, which are almost entirely mechanical, arriving at a fair spousal support arrangement is a very subjective process. What works for one couple may not work for another. The following examples are not meant to represent what the parties might have received from a judge, but rather are meant to demonstrate how different couples might settle on a fair spousal support arrangement outside of court.

The Lees (Six-Year Marriage, No Children, Low Conflict)

Sandy Lee is a successful sales representative at a high tech company in Silicon Valley. She is 33 years old, makes approximately $200,000 per year, and will likely move into a management position in the next year or two. Peter Lee is a 33-year-old high school science teacher who makes approximately $40,000 per year. The Lees have been married for six years.

Peter realizes that upon divorce he won't be able to sustain anything approaching the same standard of living he enjoyed while married. He also knows that a judge might offer him three years of spousal support. However, Peter's career is stable, his salary will increase gradually until retirement, and he doesn't want to feel like a burden to Sandy.

Likewise, Sandy wants Peter to do well but isn't thrilled about the prospect of paying him spousal support for three years. She does know, however, that Peter has always wanted to earn a master's degree to boost his salary, and several part-time programs exist which would allow Peter to earn his degree while continuing to work and accrue seniority at his job. All told, the cost of obtaining a master's degree would be approximately $20,000.

When Sandy offers to pay Peter $10,000 a year for two years to cover the expense of tuition, Peter readily accepts. The net effect of Peter's degree will be a modest increase in his standard of living. Most importantly, both Peter and Sandy are very satisfied with the compromise, and they are able to part ways as friends.

The Andersons (Nine-Year Marriage, One Child, High Conflict)

Craig and Samantha Anderson have been married for nine years. They have one child together, and Samantha has full custody of another child from a previous marriage. Craig is a 38-year-old mechanic who makes $60,000 per year, and Samantha is a 36-year-old receptionist who makes $30,000 per year. Craig and Samantha are getting divorced because of repeated infidelity, and they are having a hard time working together to settle their divorce.

Samantha is adamant about obtaining as much spousal support from her soon-to-be ex as possible, while Craig is equally adamant about not supporting Samantha any longer than necessary. Despite constant redirecting and focusing by their mediator, Craig and Samantha won't break free from their entrenched conflict. It appears that Samantha simply wants Craig to suffer, and Craig's response to this attitude is equally abrasive. He understands the concept of child support, but simply will not tolerate the idea of paying Samantha spousal support.

As is often the case in high conflict situations, a reality check is in order. The mediator reminds them that they can let a judge set spousal support after hiring two attorneys and suffering through numerous failed settlement attempts. This will ultimately cost them all of their savings and will likely result in substantial debt for both parties. Both Craig and Samantha acknowledge that this isn't what they want.

To help arrive at a fair settlement, Samantha and Craig both want to know what a judge might decide. The mediator stresses that unlike child support, spousal support is highly variable. Two different judges could easily grant very different awards of support. Yet while the amount of support varies, in California the duration of spousal support is typically half the length of a marriage of short duration. Because Samantha and Craig have been married 9 years, their marriage would most likely be considered one of short duration, and spousal support of 4.5 years would be a reasonable result. Samantha and Craig agree that fighting over the length of support is therefore a waste of time and money, and they agree on 4.5 years of spousal support.

Craig and Samantha begin to soften, and the mediator diligently tries to get them to focus on their respective needs. It becomes clear that underneath her anger, Samantha is frightened about the future, and she doesn't believe that child support combined with her salary will be enough to pay the bills. She also hopes to make the transition from receptionist to legal secretary, a career move that will increase her salary. Craig begins to realize that Samantha isn't simply trying to take him to the cleaners. She is genuinely concerned about making ends meet, and she has a plan to increase her earning capacity.

At last, Craig and Samantha begin a genuine dialogue about Samantha's true income requirements. They turn back to their respective expense declarations and run through the numbers. Craig acknowledges that in addition to paying child support (Samantha will have primary custody), he can afford to give Samantha $8,000 a year in spousal support without drastically altering his own standard of living. Samantha agrees to this figure, acknowledging that 4.5 years of support will help her "bridge the gap" to her next (ostensibly more lucrative) position.

Disaster seemed imminent at the outset of Craig and Samantha's mediation, but ultimately the couple realizes that a protracted fight only harms them both. In the end, they reach a settlement that works for both of them.

The Gersons (Twenty-Year Marriage, Two Children, Low Conflict)

Paul and Nadine Gerson have been married for twenty years and have two teenage children. Paul is a 45-year-old executive who makes $210,000 per year plus a significant yearly bonus (an average of $50,000), and Nadine is a 44-year-old stay-at-home mother. In addition to raising the children, Nadine handles the family finances and has a very good grasp of the family's assets and income.

Prior to the birth of their first child 17 years ago, Nadine worked as a flight attendant. Since then Nadine has developed a bad knee, and spending her days walking through airports or up and down the aisles of an aircraft doesn't seem like a realistic option. If she returns to work, it will have to be in an entirely new field. She previously earned an associate's degree, and would very much like to obtain a bachelor's degree.

John is resigned to the notion that Nadine will require significant spousal support. Their youngest child is 15 years old, and John and Nadine both agree that Nadine shouldn't be expected to find employment until he enters college. In the meantime, Nadine will work on attaining her bachelor's degree.

The mediator points out that because Paul makes all of the money, structuring the support payments as "family support" might be advantageous. Lumping spousal support and child support together and calling it "family support" effectively results in the entire sum being deductible for the paying spouse. However, to pass the IRS' scrutiny, the Gersons would have to be very careful about when support payments end. (You can read more about family support at the end of this chapter). The Gersons are not comfortable with the restrictions that accompany the payment of family support, and as a result, they want to split the payments between spousal support and child support.

Nadine's primary concern is her standard of living after the children leave for college. She knows that the combination of child support and alimony while the kids are around will be enough to pay the bills. However, she wants to remain in the family home after the kids are gone and pay off the mortgage (ten years of payments remain). She is rightfully skeptical of her ability to pay off the mortgage based on her income alone once she obtains a job.

Paul is sympathetic to Nadine's concerns. The thought of lifetime support makes him queasy, but he is perfectly willing to support her for a period of years. After discussing the duration of spousal support at length, Nadine and Paul both feel that ten years of support payments is reasonable. The spousal support will allow Nadine to finish her degree, get the kids off to college, find a job, and pay off the mortgage on the home. Paul will be free and clear of both child support payments and spousal support in ten years, and that gives him comfort.

Deciding on the appropriate amount of spousal support is a bit trickier, but thanks to Nadine's knowledge of the family finances and Paul's accounting acumen, they are able to pinpoint exactly how much each of them needs to maintain a reasonable lifestyle. In the end, Paul agrees to pay the following as spousal support: (a) $80,000 per year for ten years and (b) half of his yearly bonus for the next five years.

The Legal Framework for Spousal Support

The parties to a divorce are free to agree on any amount and duration of spousal support, and spouses who are willing to acknowledge each others' needs will succeed in reaching a workable compromise. Reaching a fair settlement is often aided by a general understanding of how a judge in California might approach the topic of spousal support. Unlike child support, which is almost always set by a fairly simple set of calculations, spousal support is subject to much greater discretion by the judge.

Amount

Spousal support that is paid between the date of separation and the date of divorce is called "temporary spousal support." As a rule, it is almost always higher than permanent spousal support. This is because temporary spousal support is simply calculated based on income, while permanent spousal support is calculated based upon a far broader array of criteria. Indeed, a judge will typically rely solely on a local schedule to come up with the temporary spousal support figure. Truthfully, this might be the only reasonable choice given the short amount of time a judge has to come to a decision—often a hearing of 20 to 30 minutes.

When it comes to determining the amount of permanent spousal support, a judge is not permitted to rely solely upon a schedule. To do so would be considered reversible error. Instead, a judge must consider a wide range of factors, including the income of each spouse, living expenses, the standard of living enjoyed by the couple during the marriage, the future earning capacity of each spouse, and the degree to which one spouse has contributed to the education, licensing, or training of the other. All of the factors are set forth in Section 4320 of the California Family Code (Exhibit D in the Appendix).

Notably, California courts are not permitted to consider the income provided by a new partner when calculating spousal support. This does not mean, however, that a higher earning spouse who happens to meet a wealthy new partner can stop working and therefore stop paying spousal support. While the higher earning spouse may no longer need to work to support his or her standard of living, a judge can impute income based upon the earning capacity of that spouse. In other words, a higher earning spouse's refusal to work based upon changed circumstances typically won't change the need to pay spousal support.

While linking up with a wealthier partner and declining to work won't save a paying spouse from the obligation to make support payments, a spouse who receives support should note the effect cohabiting with a new partner can have on spousal support. In California, the law presumes that when a party receiving spousal support moves in with someone of the opposite sex, his or her need for spousal support decreases. This notion is not based upon the income of the new roommate, but rather on the simple fact that sharing living expenses with another person reduces the monthly income required to sustain the same standard of living. The statutory authority for the co-habitation rule is found in Section 4320 of the California Family Code (Exhibit D in the Appendix).

Another factor that a judge will consider when setting spousal support payments is taxes. Alimony is deductible to the paying spouse and taxable to the recipient spouse as income. This can be a big advantage when one spouse earns virtually all of the income. The net effect is that the receiving spouse starts at zero and "climbs up" the income tax table. To illustrate how this can benefit both parties, consider the following example:

The Smiths

John and Jane Smith have been married for eight years. John earns $180,000 a year as a consultant, while Jane is a homemaker. Upon divorce, in addition to child support, John agrees to pay Jane spousal support of $60,000 a year for four years.

Now break out those federal tax tables and do some quick math. The amount of tax John pays (filing jointly) on $180,000 is much greater than the sum of the tax John and Jane pay (filing separately) after divorce. Filing separately, Jane must declare $60,000 as income, while John's taxable income drops to $120,000. Although the calculations will clearly vary depending on the income tax brackets in effect, the net *federal* tax savings is likely to rise to multiple thousands. Further California state tax savings will only add to the benefit.

As you might expect, a judge will consider the impact of this beneficial tax deduction to the spouse paying support when calculating a reasonable figure. This is in direct contrast to child support, which is tax neutral. In the example cited above, $60,000 a year might sound like a lot of spousal support, but the net cost to John of that support is much less thanks to the huge tax break from Uncle Sam.

Duration

When it comes to fixing the duration of spousal support, a judge has three basic alternatives:

Indefinite – This award of spousal support can't be modified unless a change of circumstances is established. It's up to the parties to seek a modification or termination. This is most commonly awarded when the parties have been married a long time (more than 10 years).

Fixed Period – This award specifies a set period of months or years for spousal support. Upon the expiration of the term, spousal support is terminated.

Conditional Termination (aka, a Richmond order) – This award terminates on a specified date unless prior to that time the recipient successfully petitions a judge to extend support. Typically a successful petition must demonstrate that certain assumptions made by the first judge never materialized (and the failure of these assumptions to materialize was not the recipient's fault). This type of award is often called a Richmond order, based on the name of the underlying case that established the concept: *Marriage of Richmond*.

The length of a marriage is by far the most important factor a judge will use when determining the duration of spousal support. In California, a marriage of over 10 years is considered a marriage of "long duration." A marriage of long duration requires either an indefinite or conditional termination award of spousal support. In special circumstances, a judge can find that a marriage of less than 10 years is a marriage of long duration as well, but this is not common.

A marriage of less than 10 years is typically known as a marriage of "short duration." A marriage of short duration requires either a fixed period award of spousal support or a conditional termination award. Prior to 1989, a judge was permitted to make an indefinite award of spousal support in a short-term marriage, but thanks to several cases, this is no longer true.

The standard period of spousal support in a marriage of short duration is one-half the length of the marriage. In other words, if the spouses were married six years, spousal support would continue for three years. The California Legislature has decreed that this is a "reasonable" amount of time for a spouse to become self-sufficient.

Effect of Loss of Employment or Reduction in Salary

First of all, as noted above, a spouse who is obligated to pay spousal support cannot reduce or eliminate support by voluntarily quitting work. A judge can react by simply imputing income to the out-of-work spouse. However, if the paying spouse is legitimately fired and is unable to find employment for many months, a judge may reduce spousal support accordingly. Likewise, if the paying spouse receives an involuntary reduction in pay, he or she can petition the court for a reduced support order.

If a paying spouse voluntarily takes a new job that involves a reduction in pay, a judge is free to impute income at the previous salary without finding that the paying spouse acted in bad faith. In one key case, a pharmacist walked away from his job to attend medical school. Even though the Court of Appeals found that his action was a good-faith attempt to increase his earning capacity, the court held that it was permissible to impute income at his prior salary for spousal support purposes. The Supreme Court of California upheld this line of reasoning. To summarize, a paying spouse who voluntarily reduces his or her income may find that a judge simply imputes income to him or her at the level previously earned.

Increasing Spousal Support

Unlike child support, an increase in the paying spouse's income has no effect on spousal support. This intuitively makes sense, as the goal of spousal support is to allow the receiving spouse to enjoy a standard of living similar to that enjoyed during the marriage. However, if the receiving spouse suffers a reduction in income or an increase in expenses and the court still has jurisdiction over the matter, it may be appropriate for a judge to increase spousal support. Of course, the party seeking modification must show a change in circumstances warranting such an increase.

A Note on Taxation – "Alimony Recapture"

As discussed earlier, due to the tax deductibility of spousal support, divorcing spouses with differing incomes have great incentive to emphasize the spousal support portion of their settlement. Worried about the potential for abuse by "front-loading" spousal support, Congress introduced alimony recapture rules in the Tax Reform Act of 1984.

Here's what you need to know: The "recapture rule" only applies to the paying spouse when alimony payments decrease substantially or end during the first three calendar years after divorce. "Decrease substantially" is defined as one of two situations: (1) When the amount paid in the third year plus $15,000 is less than the amount paid in the second year, and (2) when payments in the second and third years are averaged and this average plus $15,000 is less than the payments in the first year. If either of these scenarios occurs during the first three years, then the paying spouse will be required to "recapture" in the third post-separation year any "excess alimony" over the first and second years. The paying spouse will then have to report and pay the recaptured amount as taxable income.

Consider the following example: John Smith pays Sue Smith $50,000 in spousal support in the initial year following divorce (Year 1), $35,000 in support in the second year following divorce (Year 2), and $35,000 in support in the third year following divorce (Year 3). Applying the two tests set forth above, we calculate that (1) the amount paid in Year 3 ($35,000) plus $15,000 is more than the amount paid in Year 2 ($35,000), and (2) the average of the payments for Year 2 and Year 3 ($35,000) plus $15,000 is equal to (i.e., "not less than") the amount paid in Year 1 ($50,000).

Another example: John Smith pays Sue Smith $50,000 in spousal support in Year 1, $35,000 in Year 2, and $20,000 in Year 3. Here, the first test is satisfied because the Year 3 payment ($20,000) plus $15,000 is not more than the Year 2 payment ($35,000). However, the second test is not satisfied because the average of the payments for Year 2 and Year 3 ($27,500) plus $15,000 (a total of $42,500) is less than the payment in Year 1 ($50,000). As a result, $7,500 in spousal support is recaptured.

Keep in mind that when you calculate alimony recapture, the following payments are exempt:

- Payments made under a temporary support order.

- Payments required over a period of at least three calendar years based on a fixed percentage of income from a business, property, salary or self-employment.

- Payments that decrease because of the death of either former spouse or the remarriage of the former spouse receiving the payments.

Family Support

The "family support" concept receives shockingly little play in literature regarding divorce considering the powerful financial benefit it confers on some divorcing couples. In short, family support allows the higher-earning spouse to effectively lump child support and spousal support together in one undifferentiated payment and deduct the entire amount on his or her tax return. The entire payment amount is then taxable as income to the receiving spouse. This has the effect of reducing (possibly to a great extent) the combined tax bill for the divorcing couple. The couple can then split the difference in tax savings so they both wind up in a better position. Keep in mind, however, that family support is most useful when the difference between the salaries of each spouse is great. In particular, family support is particularly effective when one spouse isn't working.

Consider the following example to understand the tax benefits of family support: Carlos and Rosanna Pena have been married nine years and have three children. Carlos earns $80,000 a year as a computer programmer, while Rosanna is a homemaker. Instead of paying $23,000 in child support and $18,000 in spousal support, Carlos and Rosanna realize that they can benefit significantly by taking advantage of "family support." If only spousal support were deductible, Carlos would have a taxable income of $62,000, while Rosanna would have a taxable income of only $18,000 (remember that child support is not taxable to the spouse receiving the payment). Much of Carlos' income would therefore be taxed at a higher tax bracket, while Rosanna would pay virtually no tax.

However, if Carlos agrees to payments of $46,000 in family support instead of separate spousal support and child support payments, both he and Rosanna will come out ahead. Carlos now has a taxable income of only $34,000 while Rosanna has a taxable income of $46,000. Using very simplified tax calculations (each spouse claims one child, and Rosanna claims head-of-household), the net tax benefit to the two of them is approximately $2,300. In other words, Rosanna's income increases and Carlos' tax burden decreases, so that they both wind up with more money in the bank than if they opted for a traditional "alimony and child support" settlement. When finances are tight (which is almost always the case after divorce), the addition of several thousand dollars is a welcome bonus.

California Family Code Section 4066 codifies the concept of "family support" and states that "the amount of the order shall be adjusted to maximize the tax benefits for both parents." In other words, the net tax advantage of calling support "family support" should be shared by both spouses in a divorce.

To keep the IRS from challenging your family support arrangement, there are a few rules you should understand:

First, family support should be structured in a way that prevents the IRS from effectively arguing that the termination of support is tied to an event in a child's life. In the eyes of the IRS, any such termination suggests that family support is really child support in disguise. Therefore, stating that family support will terminate "on the child's eighteenth birthday" is asking for trouble. Likewise, stating that family support will end, "when the youngest child graduates from college" is likewise problematic. Instead, family support should end at least six months away from any date commonly connected to a child's life (like an eighteenth birthday or graduation from high school or college).

Second, various court cases demand that the requirement to pay family support terminates when the recipient spouse dies. In other words, any final marital separation agreement containing a family support provision should specifically state that family support terminates if and when the spouse receiving the family support payments dies.

Finally, the marital separation agreement or order containing the family support provision should clearly spell out the intended tax consequences of the family support. In other words, the document should state that the entire payment will be deductible for the paying spouse and taxable to the recipient spouse.

CHAPTER 6

Child Support

"Priority Number One"

Divorcing couples often have a much easier time settling on child support payments than spousal support. There are two reasons for this: (1) most parents acknowledge an obligation to support their children, and (2) California courts embrace a formulaic approach to calculating child support. In short, obtaining the formula-generated figure for child support often minimizes disagreement between spouses.

A court's top concern in any divorce is the welfare of the children involved. The needs of the parents will always be secondary to the needs of the children, and the inflexible nature of child support payments reflects this concern.

Here are some basic things you should know about child support in California:

- A judge will typically honor the child support figure generated by the California-mandated support formula.

- Child support is based almost entirely on the parents' incomes. Expenses are not considered.

- Child support payments continue until a child reaches majority (i.e., turns 18).

- Child support may be modified upon a change in circumstances, including an increase in income of either spouse, or a change in the child's custodial arrangement.

- Child support is tax neutral, meaning it is neither taxed as income to the receiving spouse nor deductible by the paying spouse.

Child Support, Practically Speaking

There is no greater obligation in life than the duty to support our children. This principle is woven into the very nature of our existence as human beings. Children take years to reach adulthood, and they require love and support to make the journey a smooth one. Thankfully, most parents intuitively understand and embrace this concept. The California legislature has curtailed extensive battling over child support even more by requiring the courts to apply a rigid formula when calculating the appropriate amount of support in a particular case.

For couples engaged in mediation who are committed to divorcing peacefully, child support doesn't require a great deal of discussion. The amount of support a judge would mandate is clear, and any deviation from that figure is rare. However, divorcing spouses with substantially different salaries can tap into a great gift from the State of California and the Internal Revenue Service—family support. While the concept of family support is explained in much greater detail in the previous chapter, it's worth noting that the concept represents a fine example of how some cooperative spouses can save a great deal of money in taxes by reaching an agreement outside of court.

The Legal Framework for Child Support

Subject to the requirements noted below, a divorcing couple may agree on an amount of child support that differs from the number that is generated by the statutory formula. However, the couple should be aware that if one party becomes dissatisfied with the child support figure, he or she can petition the court to modify support. The result will almost invariably be an adjustment to the level specified by the state-mandated formula.

Amount

Those who detest arithmetic may struggle with the next few pages. Keep in mind that a mediator or divorce attorney who has access to support software can easily come up with an accurate child support figure for you. Doing so is simply a matter of plugging your information into a computer program.

For those mathematically-minded individuals who want to truly understand how this works, here's the formula, as set forth in Section 4055 of the California Family Code (Exhibit B in the Appendix):

$CS = K (HN - (H\%)(TN))$
where "CS" = Child support amount
"K" = Amount of both parents' income to be allocated for child support (see below)
"HN" = High earner's net monthly disposable income
"H%" = Approximate percentage of time that the high earner has or will have primary physical responsibility for the children compared to the other parent
And TN = Total net monthly disposable income of both parties

Calculating K takes a bit of work. First, you must pick the appropriate formula from the first table on the next page. Then, you multiply the result obtained from the first formula by the appropriate formula from the second table below.

$K = 1 + H\%$ (if H% is less than or equal to 50%);

or

$K = 2 - H\%$ (if H% is greater than 50%)

The result is multiplied by the appropriate fraction from the table below to obtain K:

Total Net Disposable Income Per Month	Fraction
$0-800	0.20 + TN/16,000
$801-6,666	0.25
$6,667-10,000	0.10 + 1,000/TN
Over $10,000	0.12 + 800/TN

After K has been calculated, the rest of the formula falls into place. However, if a couple has more than one child, the total child support figure (CS) must be multiplied by the following fraction:

Number of Children	Fraction
2 children	1.6
3 children	2
4 children	2.3
5 children	2.5

6 children	2.625
7 children	2.75
8 children	2.813
9 children	2.844
10 children	2.86

This seems like a mess, doesn't it? It's not quite as complicated as it first appears and, remember, an attorney can easily generate this figure for you. Note that the rules for calculating net disposable income are set forth in Section 4059 and 4060 of the California Family Code (Exhibit B in the Appendix). For those dedicated souls who really want to understand how this all works, please consider the following examples:

The Kenneys

The Kenneys have two children. Tom Kenney's net monthly disposable income (i.e., after-tax income) is $2,500. Claire Kenney's net monthly disposable income is $6,000. They have agreed upon a 50/50 custody split for their kids. Child support is calculated as follows:

TN = $2,500 (Tom's net monthly income) + $6,000 (Claire's net monthly income)

TN = $8,500

H = 50% (or for the purposes of the formulas, the fraction 0.5)

HN = $6,000 (Claire's net monthly income)

$K = (1 + H\%)(0.10 + 1,000/TN)$

$K = (1 + 0.5)(0.10 + 1{,}000/8{,}500)$

$K = 1.5 \ (0.2176)$

$K = 0.3264$

Now plugging K into the child support formula, we have:

$CS = K \ (HN - (H\%)(TN))$

$CS = .3264 \ (\$6{,}000 - (0.5)(\$8{,}500))$

$CS = .3264 \ (\$1{,}750)$

$CS = \$571.20$

(But don't forget that because they have two children, CS must be multiplied by 1.6)

Therefore, $CS = 1.6 \ x \ \$571.20$

$CS = \$914$

In short, a judge would almost always order Claire to pay Tom $914 per month in child support.

The Penas

The Penas have three children. Felipe Pena's net monthly disposable income is $11,000. Tania Pena is a homemaker. They have agreed upon an 80/20 custody split for the kids, with Tania being the primary caretaker. Child support is calculated as follows:

$TN = \$11{,}000$ (Felipe's net monthly income, which is the total household income)

$H = 20\%$ or 0.20 (Felipe's custodial percentage)

$HN = \$11{,}000$ (Felipe's net monthly income)

$$K = (1 + H\%)(0.12 + 800/TN)$$

$$K = (1 + 0.20)(0.12 + 800/11{,}000)$$

$$K = (1.2)(.1927)$$

$$K = 0.23124$$

Now plugging K into the child support formula, we have:

$$CS = K \, (HN - (H\%)(TN))$$

$$CS = 0.23124 \, (\$11{,}000 - (0.2)(\$11{,}000))$$

$$CS = 0.23124 \, (\$8{,}800)$$

$$CS = \$2{,}034.91$$

(In this case, the Penas have three children, so CS must be multiplied by 2)

Therefore, $CS = 2 \times \$2{,}034.91$

$$CS = \$4{,}070$$

In short, a judge would almost always order Felipe to pay Tania $4,070 per month in child support. Note that in a situation like the Penas', lumping spousal support and child support together as undifferentiated "family support" would provide an enormous tax advantage. (See the end of the previous chapter for more detail).

The Rosellis

The Rosellis have one child. Anthony Roselli's net monthly disposable income is $2,000. Tricia Roselli's net monthly disposable income is $1,000. They have agreed upon 70/30 custody for the kids, with Tricia being the primary custodian. Child support is calculated as follows:

TN = $2,000 (Anthony's net monthly income) + $1,000 (Tricia's net monthly income)

TN = $3,000

H = 30% or 0.30 (Anthony's custodial percentage)

HN = $2,000 (Anthony's net monthly income)

K = (1 + H%)(0.25)   [*Note*: 0.25 comes from the income table]

K = (1.3)(0.25)

K = 0.325

Now plugging K into the child support formula, we have:

CS = K (HN - (H%)(TN))

CS = 0.325 ($2,000 – (0.3)($3,000))

CS = 0.325 ($1,100)

CS = $358

In short, a judge would almost always order Anthony to pay Tricia $358 per month in child support.

Duration

A child support order in California normally ends when the child turns 18. However, if the child is 18 but still resides at home, attends high school, and is not self-supporting, the requirement to pay child support ends when the child graduates from high school or turns 19, whichever comes first.

Section 3587 of the California Family Code (Exhibit B in the Appendix) states that a court has the authority to approve an agreement specifying the payment of child support beyond the child's 18th birthday. This is not unusual. In fact, you can agree to continue to pay child support for a set number of years after your child graduates from high school, which would almost certainly be tied to the goal of having your child obtain a bachelor's degree. Four or five years of support after graduation from high school (or until age 22 or 23) is a reasonable time period to obtain a bachelor's degree in most cases.

Agreeing Upon a Different Amount of Child Support

As noted earlier, you can always agree upon an amount of child support that differs from the figure specified by the support formula. However, before a judge can approve such an agreement, both of you must declare the following under oath or in writing:

- You both know your rights under California child support law.

- Neither of you have been subjected to coercion or duress.

- The support agreed upon is in the best interest of your minor children and will adequately meet their needs.

- The minor children are not on welfare and no application for welfare is pending.

Again, keep in mind that while you can agree on a sum below the amount dictated by the support formula, the parent receiving support can request the court to increase the support up to the formula amount without showing any change in circumstances. This is in direct contrast with a petition to modify spousal support, which requires that the parent petitioning for a different amount of support demonstrate a change in circumstances.

The Rare Exception – Court Ordered Support that Departs from the "Presumed Correct" Figure

A judge may depart from the support figure generated by a support calculator, but to do so requires the judge to find an adequate "rebuttal factor." Given the caseload faced by most courts, that is not a common occurrence. Nevertheless, "rebuttal factors" include the following:

- The paying parent's income is so high that the amount of support suggested by the support calculator would exceed the children's needs.

- The custodial parent has the benefit of living in a residence that is subject to a mortgage payment that is lower than the fair market rental value of the residence.

- A parent fails to contribute to the children's needs commensurate with that parent's allotment of time with the child.

- Application of the support formula is unjust due to special circumstances.

Use of the first potential rebuttal factor—that the paying parent's income is exceedingly high and therefore the formula generates an overly generous figure—requires that the paying parent make a very tidy income. There is no guidance in the California Family Code regarding what exactly constitutes a "very high income." The answer seems to vary from county to county and from judge to judge. In Beverly Hills, the cost of living is incredibly high, and a judge is unlikely to find someone who makes less than $80,000 *per month* a very high earner. Likewise, certain areas of the San Francisco Bay Area are subject to a comparably high threshold.

Most importantly, explaining how a child support figure that is less than the calculated amount is in the best interests of the children requires a bit of work—and judges would often rather spend their time elsewhere. Judges are reluctant to depart from the state-mandated child support formula not only because making the required factual findings takes valuable time, but also because the use of "rebuttal factors" places the judge at risk of reversal—something most judges would rather avoid. In short, persuading a judge to depart from California's child support formula is possible, but difficult.

New Spouse Income

Prior to 1994, it was widely accepted that a court could consider the income of a new spouse when computing child support payments. For example, if a father made $30,000 a year and a mother made $30,000 and custody was shared equally, no child support payments were required. (The same is true today). However, prior to 1994, if the woman subsequently married a man who made $500,000 a year, half of the new husband's income was imputed to her. The net result was that the woman owed her former husband significant child support payments.

Now, a court is expressly prohibited from considering the income of a new spouse when setting child support unless doing so is necessary to avoid "severe and extreme hardship to the children." An example of "severe and extreme hardship" might involve two parents who both earn wages that put them below the poverty level. When one of the parents remarries someone with a sizeable income, the court could declare that apportioning a percentage of the new spouse's income to child support is necessary to raise the children from the severe and extreme hardship associated with an impoverished lifestyle.

Other Child-Rearing Expenses

For some divorcing couples, the formula-generated child support figure is only the beginning. A judge may order other expenses paid in addition to the calculated amount of child support, including childcare expenses, private school tuition, health care expenses, and travel expenses incurred by the non-custodial parent.

Childcare. Childcare can be extremely expensive. Costs of up to $1,000 per month are not uncommon, and this expense is piled on top of the calculated child support figure. The question that most concerns couples is this: Who pays? The answer depends on the ratio of the spouses' net spendable incomes. Typically, the child support and spousal support a higher-earning spouse pays to the recipient spouse is sufficient to equalize their income to at least a limited extent. In that case, a judge will order that the cost of care be borne equally by both spouses. However, when one spouse has a much higher net spendable income than the other, the cost of care may be allocated proportionally.

Private school. If your children attend private school, a judge could order the payment of private school tuition on top of the calculated child support figure. Unlike families on the East Coast, Californian families tend to be more public-school oriented. If you live in a relatively prosperous neighborhood teeming with highly-educated parents, chances are the public schools are strong. Nevertheless, you may want to send your child to a school with a certain religious tradition, or perhaps you happen to live in a district in which the public schools are notoriously poor.

If both you and your spouse can agree that your children should attend a private school, it's likely that the two of you can negotiate a fair deal regarding how the cost of tuition is shared. However, if you simply can't come to an agreement, a judge will probably use the following factors to determine if a child should attend private school, and if so, who should pay: (1) the ability of the parties to pay for tuition, (2) the cost of the school, (3) the educational needs of the child, (4) the length of time the child has already attended private school, and (5) the reason why one parent wants the child to attend private school. As you might imagine, a judge is much more likely to order that a child *continue* his or her education at private school than start fresh at a new school.

Health care. The law requires that either or both parents provide health insurance for their children if it is available at no or reasonable cost. An employer-sponsored plan is considered reasonable in cost. In the absence of this option, the cost of health care is split equally unless a judge determines it is more appropriate to allocate the cost according to income.

Travel expenses. In a case decided in 1996, the California Supreme Court held that when a party moves away or relocates, he or she can be ordered to pay all of the travel costs associated with visitation by the spouse who stayed behind.

Hiding Income

Of course, if you approach your divorce like a grownup, the thought of hiding income will never cross your mind. Unfortunately, in a desperate bid to limit support payments, some parties do exactly that. Hiding income is difficult when a spouse is employed by a mid-sized to large company. However, if a spouse owns his or her own business or a professional practice, there are myriad opportunities to game the system and underreport income. Dealing in cash, hiding surplus funds inside a corporation instead of taking a full salary, and paying personal expenses out of the business coffers are just a few of the techniques desperate litigants will take to reduce the appearance of income. This concept is explored in more detail in the chapter on asset division. That said, be warned: Judges are not amused by this gamesmanship and will respond accordingly. Furthermore, the attorney and expert fees associated with playing these games almost always exceeds any reduction in support payments.

Earning Capacity

In some cases, a spouse experiences a sudden dip in income immediately prior to divorce. In some instances this is a result of being fired through no real fault of the spouse. The stress of a divorce does take its toll, and a spouse's job performance may suffer accordingly. In other cases, however, the spouse is simply trying to reduce the pool of available income a judge may consider when calculating support. Demonstrating to a judge that it was the latter motivation and not the former that caused the job loss is time-consuming and quite expensive, but it can be done.

Generally speaking, if you want to show that your spouse is not working to capacity, you will have to hire an expert in job placement who will subsequently evaluate the parent who ostensibly isn't earning enough. The expert will use his or her knowledge of the local job market for a particular skill set to determine what the spouse could reasonably expect to earn. The spouse who suffered a loss of income may be required to show a good faith effort to land a new job, and that doesn't just mean sending out hundreds of resumes. It means face-to-face interviews with potential employers. Given the high cost of hiring a job placement expert, attempting to show that a spouse isn't earning to capacity might not be a cost-effective exercise, but it may be necessary if you suspect your spouse is intentionally reducing his or her income.

CHAPTER 7

The Family Home

"Who keeps the castle?"

Determining how to handle the family home in divorce can be a daunting task. To sell or not to sell? And if the house must be sold, when?

If children are involved, simply selling the home and splitting the proceeds isn't always the most appealing option, though it's the only realistic alternative in some cases. The family home is a source of stability and comfort during the often-tumultuous divorce process for many children. Their bedroom may be their sanctuary, and the shock of realizing that their parents are separating combined with the loss of familiar surroundings can be a crippling blow.

Keep the following in mind when considering how to handle your home during divorce:

- If the family home must be sold, it doesn't necessarily have to be sold at the time of divorce.

- If one spouse brings a home into a marriage as his or her separate property, but the couple pays down the mortgage using community property funds, the community is entitled to reimbursement for those payments and may be entitled to receive a percentage of the home's appreciation.

- If the family home represents a couple's biggest asset, one spouse may "cash out" the other spouse with a promissory note.

- A judge will typically award the spouse with temporary custody of the children the right to remain in the family home in the interval between separation and divorce.

The Family Home, Practically Speaking

A home means different things to different people, but to many it symbolizes a refuge from the demands of life, a connection to the community, and the anchor of the family unit. Contemplating losing the home due to divorce is never pleasant. Depending on your situation, selling the home may not be necessary. When deciding how to deal with your home during divorce, consider the following four options, which are explored in more detail later in this chapter:

1) Buy out your spouse by purchasing his or her share of the home.

2) Sell your share of the home to your spouse.

3) Sell the house to a third party and divide the community portion of the proceeds.

4) Continue to own the home together, with the agreement that you will sell it to your spouse or a third party in the future.

As you read further, don't forget one immutable truth: negotiating a fair deal outside of court is preferable to leaving the decision of how to handle your family home to a judge. In fact, a judge won't even consider certain settlement options that might make good sense in your situation.

Valuation

Before you can reach a fair settlement regarding the family home, you must have a firm grasp of the fair market value of the residence. The current fair market value is the amount you would receive if you listed your house for sale on the open market. Obtaining a reasonably accurate figure isn't difficult if you use the appropriate channels. Real estate websites that purport to estimate the value of your home, such as zillow.com, are not nearly accurate enough for this task. That said, your local real estate agent is a valuable resource.

A real estate agent will often prepare a Comparative Market Analysis (CMA) on your property free of charge. This typically involves inspecting your home and then analyzing (1) the inventory of currently unsold homes in your neighborhood, (2) the average length of time a property takes to sell, and (3) data on the sales price of comparable homes.

If you want an even more comprehensive valuation of your home, consider hiring a real estate appraiser. The cost associated with such an appraisal can be significant (well over a thousand dollars), but if you or your spouse would rather not place your faith in the local real estate agent, a true appraisal is a good bet. Note too that if you and your spouse can't act like grownups and negotiate a fair settlement, you may end up facing a battle of appraisers. Start adding together the attorney's fees for both of you and the costs of separate appraisals, and you will quickly understand why such an approach is financially misguided.

Of course, the fair market value of your home is only the starting point in determining the equity value of your house. The equity value of a home is its fair market value minus all liabilities associated with the home, which may include any of the following:

a first, second or third mortgage, a home equity loan or a line of credit (i.e., debts to lenders), as well as property tax liens, judgment liens, mechanics' liens, and child support liens.

When determining the balance of your mortgage and/or equity loans, always use the "payoff balance" figure. The "principal balance" simply reflects the amount of principal that needs to be paid off. The "payoff balance," on the other hand, includes any prepayment charges required to settle the loan, as well as an additional month's interest.

To get a true picture of the liens on your property, you may need to do a title search. This is simply because tax liens and mechanics' liens may appear that you haven't seen before. To complete a title search, you can either enlist the help of a title company (there are many online) or make the trip to the county recorder's office and ask for the assistance of the clerk in locating your property records.

Capital Gains and Tax Basis

Depending on the difference between the price of your home when you bought it and its fair market value today, your home's tax basis may be a critically important ingredient in determining what it is truly worth to you. Many people neglect this bit of information until the time to sell the home arrives, sometimes years after a divorce, and the consequences of doing so can be harsh. Remember that in accordance with current tax law, both you and your spouse have a $250,000 capital gains exemption upon the sale of your primary residence. This total exemption amount of $500,000 is a huge benefit to married couples.

Equally importantly, you can both use your exemption toward the sale of the house if it is sold after divorce *and* you still own the home together. The IRS rule for qualifying for capital gains exclusion is that you must have occupied your home for two of the past five years. The IRS generously allows you to "tack on" the occupancy of your home by your former spouse to meet the two-year rule. Consider the following example:

Jason and Samantha Lee lived in their home for 18 months prior to divorce. According to the terms of their divorce decree, though they still co own the home, Samantha is entitled to continue residing in the home until she sells it, which she does seven months after divorce. Samantha has lived in the home for over two years, so she is clearly entitled to the $250,000 exclusion from capital gains tax. Jason, however, has only truly lived in the home for 18 months. Nevertheless, because Samantha continued to live in the home for another seven months following divorce, and the divorce decree authorizes Samantha to continue living in the home until she sells it, Jason is also eligible for the $250,000 exclusion—i.e., Samantha's extra seven months is tacked onto his occupancy for capital gains tax exclusion purposes.

None of this applies if you buy or "trade" your share of the home from your spouse. In that case, you will only be able to claim your own $250,000 capital gains exemption. Always be sure to analyze the effect that a greatly reduced exemption amount will have on your finances. Consider the following example:

Bob and Susie Ohrloff bought a lovely beach cottage in La Jolla, California in 1967 for $39,000. Over the course of the forty plus years between 1967 and the date of their divorce, the Ohrloff's little cottage appreciated significantly. In fact, at the time of their divorce, it was valued at $1.2 million. Even with the combined exemption amount of $500,000, the Orloffs would have been socked with a significant tax bill upon the sale of their residence. Indeed, approximately $700,000 of their gain would have been taxed. But Susie is very attached to the home, and she agrees to trade Bob's 50% interest in the home for its fair market value equivalent in retirement assets. In other words, Susie gets to keep the house by giving up $600,000 in retirement assets.

Unfortunately, Susie never thinks through the tax consequences of the sale. When Susie decides to sell the home and move to a retirement home five years later, she is hit with an enormous tax bill. Though the house had appreciated only slightly in value since the date of her divorce, thanks to her exemption amount of only $250,000, she now owes nearly $175,000 in capital gains taxes. Getting the cottage in exchange for surrendering her right to retirement assets doesn't seem like such a great deal after all.

To calculate the capital gains tax you will pay on your home, you need to understand the tax basis of your home. Put simply, the tax basis of your home is the original purchase price plus acquisition costs and the cost of any improvements you have made, minus certain tax benefits you've realized by owning the home. These values can be located or calculated as follows:

- The *purchase price* should be located on your closing statement. If you can't find your closing statement (or contract), contact the lender who handled your mortgage.

- *Acquisition costs* include title insurance, recording fees, and document fees. These costs do not include loan interest. These figures should be on your escrow or closing statement.

- *Capital improvements* are changes you've made to your home that positively affect its value, such as remodeling the kitchen, adding a fourth bedroom, or finishing the attic. Other examples include constructing a swimming pool, putting in new windows, installing a security system, or building a new fence around the property. Hopefully you have kept careful records of the expenses associated with improving your home—if nothing else, a shoebox full of receipts, cancelled checks or old credit card statements may suffice.

- The *tax benefits* you need to subtract from the tax basis calculation include any rollover gain from the sale of a prior residence before August 1999, together with any depreciation you have taken for use of your residence as a home office. When in doubt, consult with an accountant.

When property is transferred from one spouse to another as part of a divorce settlement, the original tax basis is transferred to the spouse receiving the property. The capital gains tax on the property when it is subsequently sold is calculated using this basis.

Total Housing Costs

The next step in the process of deciding how to handle your home during divorce involves calculating your total housing cost per month. Use the chart below to calculate your gross housing cost per month, which is the sum total of all expenses related to living in your home.

Expense	Cost
Mortgage	$_____
Home Equity Loan Payment/ Second Mortgage	$_____
Property Tax	$_____
Maintenance*	$_____
Insurance	$_____
Homeowner's Association Fees	$_____
Utilities	$_____

Homeowner's Insurance	$_____
Total	$_____

* When totaling your maintenance costs, don't forget to include such things as house cleaning, lawn care/gardening, pool care, pest control, painting, plumbing and other repairs.

This exercise should make it clear that the cost of owning and maintaining a home far exceeds the amount of your mortgage payment.

After you've come up with a figure for your gross housing cost, find your *net* housing cost by subtracting out any tax benefit you receive from home ownership. The Form 1099 that you receive at the end of each year will show how much you paid in mortgage interest. Under current law you can deduct that amount, together with all property taxes paid, on your federal tax return.

Calculating your tax savings is simple enough. Simply add your property tax bill to the total amount of interest paid on your mortgage during the year. Next multiply this number by your tax bracket, and then divide by 12 to get a monthly average.

To obtain your net housing cost, subtract your tax savings from your gross housing costs. Now you should have a fair sense of how much it costs you to live in your home each month. The example below illustrates how these calculations might work:

Sue and John Smith own a home worth $400,000. Their mortgage payments total $1,200 per month (they've owned the home for 15 years, and it has appreciated rapidly). Their Form 1099 shows that they paid $7,000 in mortgage interest last year, and their property tax bill was $2,400. Their federal tax bracket is 25%, and their net gross housing costs (including maintenance, insurance, etc.) are $2,400 monthly, or $28,800 annually.

First, to calculate their tax savings, simply add their mortgage interest payment and their property tax bill and then multiply this figure by their tax bracket:

($7,000 + $2,400) x 0.25 = $2,350

Next, simply subtract their tax savings from their annual gross housing costs to obtain their net annual housing cost:

$28,800 – $2,350 = $26,450

Finally, divide this number by 12 to get the Smith's net monthly housing cost:

$26,450/12 = $2,204

The Decision

The three figures previously discussed—the equity value of your home, its tax basis, and your net monthly housing cost—will help you decide what to do with your home upon divorce. The equity value of your home and its tax basis are extremely important when it comes to analyzing the amount you would realize on the sale of the home in various scenarios. Your net monthly housing cost provides a valuable benchmark when calculating the value of staying in your home versus selling it.

Calculating Gain

The equity value of your home minus any real estate agent commissions, closing costs, and capital gains tax is roughly the gain you and your spouse would expect to realize if it were sold for fair market value. For example, if your home has a net equity value of $300,000, real estate agent commissions and closing costs amount to $10,000, and you will owe no capital gains tax upon the sale of the home, you can expect to divide $290,000.

The tax basis of your home is a critical element used to determine the capital gains tax implications of various methods of dealing with your home. If the tax basis of your home is sufficiently low, you may have to grapple with capital gains. Of course, if you meet the occupancy requirement and the fair market value of your home minus the tax basis of your home is less than $250,000, capital gains calculations aren't important. Your home will not be subject to tax upon sale. However, if the fair market value of your home minus the tax basis of your home is more than $250,000, the manner in which you deal with your home during divorce can have important tax consequences. As discussed previously, selling your home during the divorce process (or afterward if you still own it with your former spouse and this is noted in your divorce decree) will give you the benefit of a $500,000 exemption. If you are single and your spouse no longer retains any ownership of the home, selling your home after the divorce process will only give you a $250,000 exemption.

Before diving into the calculations that will tell you how much money you will make upon the sale of your home (if any), you need to learn one new term and refresh your memory regarding a few others.

> *"Cost of Sale"* is the sum of all real estate agent commissions and closing costs.

> *"Fair Market Value"* is what your home is worth on the date of sale.

> *"Net Equity Value"* is the fair market value of your home minus any liabilities associated with the home (mortgage, home equity loan, etc.)

"Exemption Amount" is (a) $500,000 if your home is sold during the divorce process, after the divorce if you co-own the property with your spouse, or after subsequent remarriage, or (b) $250,000 if your home is sold after the divorce and you are single.

"Percentage Ownership" is exactly what you would expect. It is the amount of the home that you "own," including your half interest in the community property portion of the home as well as any separate property interest in the home. Determining your percentage ownership in the home can be tricky if either you or your spouse acquired the home before marriage. If this applies to you, carefully read pages 133-138 under "The Legal Framework" below.

"Tax Rate" is simply the rate at which you will be taxed on any capital gain. As of the writing of this book, long-term capital gains tax rates are 15% for taxpayers in the 25% and higher income brackets, and 5% for taxpayers in the 10% and 15% tax brackets.

"Tax Basis" is explained in detail earlier in this chapter.

Now, calculate the amount of money you can expect to receive if you sell your home using the following steps:

Step 1: *Calculate the capital gains tax that will be due upon sale.*

Capital Gains Tax = [[(Fair Market Value) – (Tax Basis) – (Cost of Sale) – (Exemption Amount)] x (Tax Rate)]

Step 2: *Calculate the total gain from the sale.*

Gain = (Net Equity Value) – (Cost of Sale) – (Capital Gains Tax)

Step 3: *Calculate your share of the gain.*

Amount Realized = (Gain) x (Percentage Ownership)

Example: Manny and Rosa Ramirez just finished paying off the mortgage on their home, which now has a fair market value of $700,000 and net equity value of $700,000. The tax basis of the Ramirez's home is $150,000. Manny's combined community property and separate property share of the home is 75% (he owned the home prior to marriage). Real estate commissions and closing costs upon the sale of the home (i.e., the Cost of Sale) total $30,000. The current capital gains rate applicable to the Ramirez's sales of their home is 15%. The benefit of selling the house now for Manny is calculated as follows:

Step 1:

Capital Gains Tax Due = [(Fair Market Value) – (Tax Basis) – (Cost of Sale) – (Exemption Amount)] x (Tax Rate)

Capital Gains Tax Due = [($700,000) – ($150,000) – ($30,000) – ($500,000)] x (.15)

Capital Gains Tax Due = $3,000

Step 2:

Gain = (Net Equity Value) – (Cost of Sale) – (Capital Gains Tax)

Gain = ($700,000) – ($30,000) – ($3,000)

Gain = $667,000

Step 3:

Amount Realized = (Gain) x (Percentage Ownership)

Amount Realized = ($667,000) x (.75)

Amount Realized = $500,250

In other words, Manny will receive $500,250 if the Ramirez's residence is sold during the divorce process.

To calculate the amount he would realize upon sale of the residence if he traded his wife's 25% stake in the home for other assets and subsequently sold the home two years later, we should make some assumptions about how the home will appreciate (or depreciate) during those two years. For the sake of simplicity, let's just assume that the housing market has flattened completely, so the Ramirez's home does not change in value at all during the intervening two-year period. Therefore, the amount realized by Manny when he sells the home two years after the divorce is calculated as follows:

Step 1:

Capital Gains Tax Due = [(Fair Market Value) − (Tax Basis) − (Cost of Sale) − (Exemption Amount)] x (Tax Rate)

Capital Gains Tax Due = [($700,000) − ($150,000) − ($30,000) − ($250,000)] x (.15)

Capital Gains Tax Due = $40,500

Step 2:

Gain = (Net Equity Value) − (Cost of Sale) − (Capital Gains Tax Due)

Gain = ($700,000) − ($30,000) − ($40,500)

Gain = $629,500

Step 3:

Amount Realized = (Gain) x (Percentage Ownership)

Amount Realized = ($629,500) x (1.00)

Amount Realized = $629,500

The important figure for basis of comparison is the gain (underlined above). While Manny gets to keep 100% of the proceeds of the sale because he traded other assets for full ownership of the house, the total gain from selling the property is almost $40,000 less than if he had sold the property together with his wife. This decrease is solely due to increased capital gains tax. Let's hope Manny factored the increased tax burden into his calculations when he traded other property for full ownership of the home.

Current Net Housing Costs and Expectations

Once you've figured out how much you can expect to realize from the sale of your home, you need to take stock of your financial situation and decide what you can afford. This is when knowing your net monthly housing costs is invaluable. Analyzing your net monthly housing costs will give you a quick sense of the benefit of remaining in the home, as well as a little perspective when it comes to housing possibilities. Consider your current net monthly housing costs an important benchmark. For most divorcing couples, dividing up the community property and potentially shifting from a two-income household to a one-income household means that each spouse should look for housing that is far cheaper than their current net monthly housing costs.

Do a little market research, and think hard about where you hope to live in a few years. Will you be moving to a less expensive neighborhood, downsizing, or otherwise reducing your standard of living? (Depending on your financial situation, you may not have a choice.) Will you be moving to the city and renting that cozy apartment you've always dreamed about, or will you buy a piece of land in the countryside and build yourself a cottage? Or, as is often the case, will you try to resettle in a more modest residence a short distance away?

For couples who purchased their home years ago in an area that has seen significant appreciation, current net housing costs may be even lower than the rent one of them could expect to pay after divorce. If you find yourself in this situation, staying in the house is a good bet, provided you can convince your spouse to sell his or her one-half share to you. Couples with children often have an extra incentive to allow one spouse to remain in the home—it provides a nice sense of stability to the children, who are already undoubtedly grappling with the abrupt life changes that have been foisted upon them.

The Four Options

Option 1: Buy out your spouse by purchasing his or her share of the home.

If you have children, this is often the ideal option. Remember, though, that after you buy out your spouse's share of the property, your capital gains exclusion drops to $250,000. For many individuals, this simply isn't an issue—the home hasn't appreciated enough. For others, it's a worthy consideration. Tens of thousands of dollars in taxes can be saved by selling the residence while it is co-owned by both spouses.

If you do decide to buy out your spouse's share of the home, you may wonder how in the world you can afford to do that. After all, the family residence is the most significant asset for a majority of couples in California. If simply giving up other community property assets, such as stocks and bonds or an interest in a retirement plan, is enough to offset your spouse's interest in the house, that may be a simple solution. An equally appealing option presents itself to those fortunate individuals who own a significant amount of separate property. If you fall into this category, consider simply buying out your spouse by transferring some of the separate property to him or her.

For many divorcing individuals who wish to buy out their spouse's share of the family home, something more creative is required. Although there are many possible approaches, here are a few of the more common tactics you might consider:

- *Refinance the house or take out a second mortgage and pay the proceeds to your spouse.* Depending on market conditions and the amount of equity you have built up in your home, simply refinancing your mortgage might generate enough cash to allow you to buy-out your spouse's interest. If not, a second mortgage on the home might do the trick. Interest payments made on the second mortgage are usually tax deductible.

- *Use an installment loan.* If you plan to remain in the home, ask your spouse if he or she would be willing to accept a secured installment note specifying payments over a fixed period of time in exchange for surrendering his or her interest in the home. Securing the note with the home affords your spouse some protection in the event that you default on the note. Furthermore, the interest you pay on the note may be deductible in the same way that mortgage interest is tax deductible.

- *Surrender your right to alimony payments.* If it's likely that a judge would require your spouse to pay you a significant amount of alimony, offer to give up your right to receive some (if not all) of these payments in exchange for your spouse's share of the home.

- *Enter into an equity share financing arrangement.* You may also want to consider asking your spouse to sell his or her share of the home to a third party—typically a relative or friend of yours. If this approach seems appealing, you may want to engage the help of a financial professional to make sure you comply with IRS rules and enjoy all available tax benefits. You will also want to ensure that you draft an agreement that clearly spells out your rights and the third party's rights. In most cases you would be required to pay rent to your new co-owner, simply because only you would have current enjoyment of the residence.

Option 2: Sell your share of the home to your spouse.

This is simply the inverse of Option 1. The mechanics are the same. Since in this scenario you are selling your share of the home, be sure that if your spouse offers you a promissory note in exchange for your equity interest in the home, the note is secured by the home itself.

Option 3: Sell the house to a third party and divide the community portion of the proceeds.

For many couples, this is the simplest option. For others, due to limited finances or a relatively expensive mortgage, it is simply the only feasible option. It has the great advantage of making the division of the home extremely simple. If your home is 100% community property, you can simply split the cash proceeds from the sale equally.

Option 4: Continue to own the home together, with the agreement that you will sell it to your spouse or a third party in the future.

If you have teenagers, you may simply want to offer them the stability of continuing to live in the family home while they are still in high school. Once they are safely off at college, perhaps you want to downsize. You and your spouse can agree that you will remain in the home with the kids until the youngest is in college, at which point you will sell the home and split the proceeds.

While this sounds simple enough, this option has several disadvantages. Apportioning responsibility for upkeep, repairs, improvements, and taxes can create conflict. Ultimately both spouses will split the proceeds from the sale, but only one spouse is currently enjoying the benefit of residing in the home. As a result, spouses who continue to own a home together should create a clear written agreement setting forth the rules regarding who covers each category of expenses.

In addition, continuing to own a home together requires a bit of thought with regard to estate planning. Clearly you will no longer hold the home as community property, as doing so requires being married. So what happens if the spouse with whom you co-own the house passes away before the anticipated date of sale? If you held the home as joint tenants, you will suddenly find yourself with full ownership of the home. This might sound nice; however, keep in mind that if you die, the opposite is true—your spouse will end up with 100% ownership of the home. Either you or your spouse might have different beneficiaries whom you would like to provide for when you die. Joint tenancy does not allow this.

Holding the home as tenants in common has the advantage of allowing each of you to leave your one-half interest in the home to your chosen beneficiaries if you die before the home sells. However, keep in mind that the beneficiaries may indeed force a sale before you are ready to move out. They may not want to sit around and wait to collect on their inheritance.

The solution? You have a few options. First, if you wish to continue living in the home after your former spouse dies, consider taking out a life insurance policy on his or her life. This will allow you to buy out the interest held by your former spouse's beneficiaries. Second, you can ask an attorney to draw up an agreement outlining your rights and responsibilities with respect to your co-ownership of the home. This agreement would address what should happen to the home if he or she dies while you are still living in it.

The Legal Framework of the Family Home

The family home is either community property or separate property depending on when it was acquired. As discussed in Division of Assets and Debts, property acquired before marriage or by "gift, bequest, devise, or descent" is characterized as separate property. Property acquired during the marriage is community property.

Calculating Each Spouse's Share of the Home

In many instances, one spouse enters the marriage already owning a home as his or her separate property. Over the course of the marriage the couple then pays down the mortgage using community property funds. To determine how much of the home's value is attributable to community property, California courts rely on two important cases.

With *In re Marriage of Mardsen* and *In re Marriage of Moore,* California courts established the calculations used to apportion a percentage of a home acquired prior to marriage to the community property of husband and wife. In *Moore,* the court held that the married couple's payment of taxes and interest on a home during the course of the marriage should not be considered when calculating the community property interest in the home. In other words, only the married couple's payment of loan principal during the marriage effectively increases the percentage share of the home that is considered community property.

According to the *Moore* case, a simple ratio is established between the amount of principal that was paid with separate property funds and the amount of principal that was paid with community property funds. The court in *Moore* goes on to state that the separate property percentage interest is determined by crediting the separate property with the down payment and the full amount of the loan less the amount by which the community property payments reduced the balance of the loan. This sum is then divided by the purchase price. The result is the separate property percentage share in the property. The community property percentage interest is found by dividing the amount by which community property payments reduced the principal by the purchase price.

Consider the following example, which demonstrates how a court would apply the *Moore* formula:

Sue Smith bought a house for the price of $100,000 in 2001. She made a down payment of $20,000 on the property. Between the date of the purchase and her marriage to John (in 2002), she made additional principal payments in the amount of $2,000. John and Sue file for divorce in 2010. During the course of their marriage (2002 to 2010), they used community property funds to pay down an additional $18,000 in principal.

According to the *Moore* formula, Sue's separate property interest in the home is calculated as follows:

1) First, the full down-payment amount ($20,000) is added to the full amount of the loan ($80,000).

   $20,000 to $80,000 = $100,000 (i.e., the purchase price)

2) Second, the community's principal payments ($18,000) are subtracted from the result of Step 1.

$100,000 - \$18,000 = \$82,000$

3) Third, the result of Step 2 is then divided by the original purchase price to obtain Sue's percentage ownership.

$\$82,000/\$100,000 = 82\%$

4) Lastly, the community property percentage ownership is calculated by dividing the principal payments made by the community by the total purchase price.

$\$18,000/\$100,000 = 18\%$

In *Marriage of Mardsen*, the court "adjusted" the formula used in *Moore* by stating that a court may consider the premarital appreciation of the home when determining the percentage interests in the home that should be considered community property and separate property. In *Mardsen*, the husband had purchased the home approximately nine years before marriage, during which time the property had appreciated significantly. The court wrote:

> Where the separate property is owned for a considerable period before marriage, the increase in value in an inflationary market, such as we have had for the past several decades, is substantial. The fair market value at the time of marriage would usually be significantly greater than the purchase price, and this is true of the case before us. We think it is equitable to credit the separate property interest with this prenuptial appreciation.

Here is a slight variation on the previous example, which demonstrates how the court would calculate the separate property interest based on the holding of *Mardsen*:

Sue Smith bought a home for the price of $100,000 in 2001. She made a down-payment of $20,000 on the property and took out a mortgage of $80,000. Between the date of the purchase and her marriage to John (in 2005), she made an additional $10,000 in principal payments. John and Sue file for divorce in 2010. During the course of their marriage (2005 to 2010), they used community funds to pay down an additional $12,000 in principal. The fair market value of the property on the date of the marriage was $130,000. The fair market value of the property at the time of the trial was $160,000.

According to the *Mardsen* case, Sue's separate property interest in the home is calculated as follows (note that Steps 1 through 3 simply follow the *Moore* formula):

1) The full down-payment amount ($20,000) is added to the full amount of the loan ($80,000).

   $20,000 to $80,000 = $100,000

2) The community's principal payments ($12,000) are subtracted from the result of Step 1.

   $100,000 − $12,000 = $88,000

3) The result of Step 2 is then divided by the original purchase price to obtain Sue's percentage ownership.

   $88,000/$100,000 = 88%

4) The appreciation in the value of the property before marriage is calculated by subtracting the purchase price of the home from the fair market value of the home at the time of marriage.

   $130,000 - $100,000 = $30,000

5) Sue's fractional interest in the appreciation during the marriage is calculated by multiplying the total appreciation during the marriage by Sue's percentage interest in the home.

$30,000 x 0.88 = $26,400

6) The total amount of appreciation before marriage is added to Sue's fractional interest in the appreciation during the marriage (the result of Step 5).

$26,400 + $30,000 = $56,400

7) Sue's total separate property interest in the home is calculated by adding her total principal payments prior to marriage (down-payment of $20,000 plus additional principal payment of $10,000) to the result of Step 6.

$30,000 + $56,400 = $86,400

8) The community property interest in the appreciation during the marriage is calculated by multiplying the total appreciation during the marriage by the community property percentage interest in the home.

$30,000 x 0.12 = $3,600

9) Finally, the community property interest in the appreciation during the marriage (the result of Step 8) is added to the total amount of principal payments made using community property funds.

$12,000 + $3,600 = $15,600

A quick check shows that this calculation works, as Sue's separate property interest ($86,400) plus the community's interest ($15,600) equals $102,000, which also happens to equal the fair market value at the time of trial ($160,000) minus the remaining amount payable on the mortgage ($58,000).

All told, Sue therefore is entitled to all of her separate property interest in the home ($86,400) plus half of the community's interest in the home ($15,600/2 = $7,800), for a total of $94,200.

John is therefore only entitled to half of the community property interest, or $7,800.

Deferring Sale of the Family Home

Remember, you and your spouse can agree upon a wide range of possibilities when it comes to structuring the dissolution of your marriage. However, if you opt to litigate and ultimately leave the decision of what to do with the family home to a judge, the range of possible outcomes is restricted. When in doubt, assume the home will be sold.

In a 1980 Court of Appeals case *In re Marriage of Duke*, California courts were given the option of deferring the sale of the family home for the benefit of the children. However, a judge's ability to defer was subsequently restricted by a different case in 1987, which stated that expert psychiatric or psychological testimony regarding the necessity of the deferral was required. The legislature then stepped in and expressly permitted California courts to defer the sale of the family home, provided that the court found that doing so was economically feasible. In addition, the legislature indicated that the deferral may be considered part of the child support award.

Before granting a deferral, a judge must therefore grapple with the question of what "economically feasible" means in a particular case. Essentially, the judge analyzes the ability of the non-custodial parent to find decent housing, the degree to which the delay in selling the home will cause the non-custodial parent financial harm, and the tax consequences involved. All these factors are weighed against the impact the immediate sale of the home would have on the children, as well as the impact the loss of the home would have on the custodial parent's ability to continue working at his or her present job.

Predicting whether or not a particular judge will grant deferral is difficult. In general, though, a judge is unlikely to defer the sale of a home until the youngest child graduates from high school if that child recently entered kindergarten. Indeed, most deferrals are for a short fixed period. Note that a judge will also typically refuse to grant a deferral unless the children have some reason to be attached to the residence—i.e., the children have lived there for at least four years.

Remember that a judge is not solely concerned with the custodial parent's welfare. The ability of the noncustodial parent to adequately host the children at his or her home is also critical. If a deferral would make it impossible for the non-custodial parent to afford a big enough home to house the kids during visits, a judge won't grant the deferral.

Living in the House Prior to Divorce

If you are able to peaceably negotiate your divorce, you can make the best decision possible regarding who (if anyone) gets to remain in the family home. However, in the event that litigation seems likely, you need to understand your rights when it comes to remaining in the house.

In the absence of a physically or emotionally threatening environment, both spouses are entitled to continue to reside in the family residence after a divorce petition is filed. Of course, if the situation is volatile enough to require the court to intervene, permitting both spouses to remain in the home isn't a realistic option—something a judge fully understands. All too often this results in a race to court, with each spouse vigorously attempting to persuade the judge to throw the other out of the family home.

First of all, it's relatively easy for a judge to come to the conclusion that emotional harm will befall the parties if they remain together in the home. A contested divorce is ugly enough without two spouses trying to share common space. The question then becomes who gets to stay in the home. If children are involved, the answer is easy. The spouse with temporary support of the children gets to stay in the home. (Of course, if both spouses share time with the children equally, i.e. a 50/50 temporary custody arrangement—the situation is complicated somewhat.)

What if the situation is really out-of-hand and one spouse needs to exclude the other on an emergency basis? Well, then a judge must come to a decision based on declarations under oath, a very unreliable form of evidence. Making baseless exaggerations is far too easy when parties aren't required to appear in court and face a judge. As a result, many judges require actual evidence of physical violence before any such order is granted. A simple threat of violence may not be enough.

Typically a few hours notice is required before a spouse can be forced out of the residence, but a judge can dispense with this requirement if such notice is likely to incite violence. In short, simply remember that to get your spouse out of the house immediately, you will have to prove that you and/or your children are truly at risk.

Watts Claims and Epstein Credits – To Stay or Leave?

If the fair market value of your home doesn't match the sum of your mortgage payments, taxes, and insurance, allowing one spouse to remain in the home before a divorce is finalized can get complicated. If you have lived in your home for many years, it's entirely possible that the sum of your mortgage payments, taxes, and insurance is significantly less than the amount you might receive if you rented the home. Unfortunately for the spouse who stays in the home, a debt is created in favor of the spouse who leaves. Put simply, the spouse who leaves is entitled to claim a right to reimbursement for half of the difference between the fair market rental value of the home and the sum of the mortgage payments, taxes, and insurance on the home. This is known as a *Watts* claim, and is named after the case that established the concept. Of course, a trial judge has the discretion to deny a *Watts* claim, but you should always be aware that facing such a claim is a very real possibility. To understand how a *Watts* claim works, consider the following example:

John and Sue Smith decide that Sue should remain in the house as they sort out their divorce. They bought their house twenty years ago, and as a result, the combination of mortgage payments, taxes, and insurance is a modest $2,000 per month. Fair market rent for the home is $3,500 per month. Sue remains in the residence, unaware that she is accruing a debt to John on the order of $750 per month, which is half of the difference between fair market rent ($3,500) and the current mortgage payments, taxes, and insurance ($2,000). Sue and John take their time getting divorced, and Sue remains in the home alone for 22 months before a decree is issued. Sue is later shocked when she discovers that she is liable to John for $16,500!

The inverse of a *Watts* claim can also be problematic, but this time it is the spouse who leaves who gets penalized. Imagine a situation in which a couple has refinanced their home to the hilt, and their total mortgage payments, taxes, and insurance vastly exceed the fair market rental value of their home. Assume the spouse who remains in the home accepts responsibility for paying the mortgage, taxes, and insurance. In this case, the spouse who leaves may owe a credit to the spouse who stays equal to the difference between the sum of the mortgage payments, taxes, insurance and the fair market rental value of the home. This is called an *Epstein* credit, and is named after the case that established the concept. To understand how an *Epstein* credit works, consider the following example:

Carlos and Anna Lopez have struggled financially, and they've borrowed heavily against their home. As a result of refinancing several times and taking out a second mortgage, they make monthly payments of $4,000 to cover their two mortgages, property tax, and insurance. The fair market rental value of their home is $2,000 per month. Pending a divorce decree, Anna remains in the home for six months with the children, while Carlos rents an apartment. Much to Carlos' surprise, he owes Anna half of the difference between the sum of the mortgage payments, taxes, and insurance ($4,000) and the fair market rental value of the home ($2,000) for that six-month period. Had Carlos known he would owe Anna $6,000, he would have thought twice about their housing arrangements while they waited for a final divorce decree.

CHAPTER 8

Custody

"Honor Your Children"

Divorce by itself is heart-wrenching, and the addition of children to the equation makes it even more challenging. If a couple doesn't have children, and they insist on dragging their divorce into court and litigating away much of their savings, at least the victims of the damage they inflict are adults. Sadly, when minor children are involved, the emotional harm resulting from a high conflict divorce may last for many years. Indeed, many now-middle-aged individuals who endured a high conflict divorce when they were children still consider it the most painful and scarring experience of their lives.

Sound intimidating? Take heart in the fact that millions of divorced parents have navigated their way through the process while making their children's emotional welfare their top priority. This is well-traveled territory, and with some careful planning, good intentions, and a strong heart, you can not only survive the process, but you can also ensure that your children are raised in a stable, loving environment. When sorting out custody, the key to success involves that same tired refrain—*act like a grownup*. Your children need you to behave—desperately. If you can't compose yourself and act with dignity for your own sake, do it for theirs.

If the negotiation process breaks down and you and your spouse simply can't agree on who should care for your children, you will undoubtedly wind up in court. As noted elsewhere in this book, family court judges are exceedingly busy. While resolving custody disputes is a very important part of their job, judges simply don't have the time or the insight into the details of your children's lives to make a "perfect" decision, if such a thing exists. You can take heart in the fact that judges really do their best to look out for the interests of your children, but you can also be sure you will achieve a better result by using a mediator to resolve custodial conflict.

If you simply can't resolve the issue of how responsibility for taking care of the children should be shared, you should skip ahead to the section titled "The Legal Framework for Custody." There you will find a description of how a judge and/or a court-appointed custody evaluator will decide who should care for your children. Before you throw in the towel, though, please do everything in your power to work with your spouse to resolve your issues. It's better for your children, and it's better for you.

Here are a few basic things you need to know about child custody:

- If a couple can't reach agreement on custody, a mental health professional known as a custody evaluator, not a judge, typically decides how custody will be shared.

- Before a judge makes anything more than a temporary award of custody or visitation, California law requires spouses to mediate their differences.

- Most judges would consider a child's degree of attachment to each parent the most important factor in evaluating custodial arrangements.

- The law governing whether a custodial parent may relocate children out of state has changed repeatedly, and it is now almost impossible for a noncustodial parent to prevent relocation.

144

Custody, Practically Speaking

<u>Understand the Basics – Legal Custody vs. Physical Custody</u>

The term *physical custody* refers to the parent (or both parents, if custody is shared) who has physical responsibility for the care of the children. The term *legal custody* refers to the parent (or both parents, if custody is shared) who will possess decision-making authority relating to the health, education, and welfare of a child.

The term *joint physical custody* is often misused in California. It does not mean equal time-sharing, as many seem to believe. Indeed, a parent who only sees his or her children every other weekend and a few weeks during the summer may be awarded joint physical custody. This has the benefit of avoiding the term "visitation." No parent wants to feel like a visitor when spending time with his or her own children. The term *sole physical custody* simply means that one parent has the right to have the children live with him or her.

Although the term *primary physical custody* is not defined anywhere in the Family Code, family courts continue to use the term. This can have a significant impact when one spouse wants to relocate the children. If that spouse has sole physical custody or even primary physical custody, he or she may be permitted to leave with the kids without the permission of the other spouse (see "Moving Children Away" below). When dealing with percentages, a spouse who has custody of the children less than 45% of the time may be in danger of helplessly watching them leave.

Joint legal custody means that both parents have the authority to make decisions regarding the health, education, and welfare of the children. This involves determining whether or not they should attend church, where they should attend school, and when they should be able to obtain a driver's license. *Sole legal custody* means that one parent has the authority to make all of these decisions.

145

How You Can Help Your Children

If you haven't yet achieved a sense of peace regarding the fact that you are headed for divorce, you may struggle to project the sense of strength and calm that your children crave. Indeed, you may be struggling through the first stage of divorce for many individuals: denial. Pretending nothing is wrong and refusing to acknowledge where things are headed will not benefit your children. Unless they are very young (i.e., less than three years old), chances are they are acutely aware of the tension between you and your spouse, and they may know that divorce is likely. Don't shield your children from the truth, but do insulate them from your "adult" problems. They don't need to know that your spouse slept with a coworker, or that he or she wants to financially destroy you. They do need to know that you love them, unconditionally, and that while you *are* beginning the painful divorce process, none of this is their fault.

Also, as you begin negotiating custody arrangements with your spouse, try your hardest to turn off the calculator in your head that starts equating increased custody with lower child support payments, or vice versa. Undoubtedly you love your children, and try to remember that creating a good custody plan requires you to put their interests first. Some financially savvy spouses (particularly breadwinners in one-income families) will fight for increased custody so that their support payments decrease. In the end, this game always backfires. The parent who fought so hard for a higher percentage of physical custody in the interest of reducing child support often finds that the reality of caring for the children is overwhelming.

The most painful reality of all when it comes to custody is that some parents simply shouldn't push for more time with the children. We have been programmed to believe that we should do everything perfectly: be the perfect employee, the perfect friend, the perfect parent. A palpable sense of shame often accompanies the admission that caring for the children every other week is simply too much.

Honest introspection will always serve you well. Look deeply inside yourself and ask whether you truly have the capacity to care for your children half of the time. If your spouse is floundering, you may not have a choice (indeed, you may end up with sole physical custody). In that case, you should reach out for parenting support from as many sources as possible. But if your spouse is a stellar parent, and you feel overwhelmed with the task of caring for your children half of the time, you need to consider alternate custodial arrangements. Admitting that your spouse may be better suited to the critical task of child rearing is not an admission of defeat, though it may feel like one. It's simply being realistic, and honestly assessing your own skill set is a powerful first step in establishing a suitable custodial arrangement.

Developing a Parenting Plan – Core Issues

1) Where will the children live?

Deciding where your children will live after your divorce is perhaps the most critical decision you will make during the settlement process. This decision not only involves the basic question of whether they will live in one residence or split their time between two homes, but naturally also involves how much time they will spend with each parent. There are several possible approaches with regard to housing your children, and they include (a) one home, (b) dual homes, (c) someone else's home, and (d) one home on a time-share basis.

One Home

For many children, picking one home as the primary residence makes good sense. Young children in particular may thrive on the routine and familiarity associated with a single home. Having one bedroom, one set of clothes, one chest full of toys, and one set of neighborhood playmates may add stability to their lives. Of course, having one primary home has disadvantages as well. The importance of the relationship between the noncustodial parent and the children may be diminished over time. In addition, the children may feel like visitors when they travel to the noncustodial parent's home for the weekend.

Another potential challenge of having the children primarily reside in one home is that the noncustodial parent may start to fall into the role of the "fun" parent. While the custodial parent is saddled with the unglamorous tasks associated with day-to-day living (changing diapers, shuttling kids to soccer practice and music lessons, doling out discipline, etc.), the noncustodial parent focuses solely on having a good time with the kids. This can arise from the noncustodial parent's overpowering desire to have the children like him or her despite the limited interaction between them. It can also arise from the noncustodial parent's desire to cram as much activity into one weekend as possible (making up for lost time). Sadly, it can also result from laziness. Disciplining kids and shaping them into responsible human beings takes a lot of love and a lot of work. Caving in is easier, particularly when the noncustodial parent assumes the other parent is taking care of the essentials.

The custodial parent may begin to resent the fact that the kids return home from their "fun weekend" with tales of adventure, staying up late, watching movies, and jumping on the bed. It may take a few days for the children to settle back into their normal routine. A responsible noncustodial parent will be conscious of the

148

responsibility associated with his or her role. Fun is important—true. But so is being a real parent who contributes in meaningful ways to the children's development.

Custodial arrangements involving one primary home can take on a number of forms. A few of the more common arrangements are as follows:

- *Alternating weekends* (Friday night to Saturday night). For parents who live in reasonably close proximity to one another, this custody arrangement is often viewed as the minimal amount of time the noncustodial parent should spend with the children. Four overnights in a one-month period is not a lot, and the children may feel themselves drifting away from the noncustodial parent. This arrangement also has the disadvantage of allowing the custodial parent very limited (if any) involvement in school and extracurricular activities. Lastly, the custodial parent doesn't get much of a break from the relentless task of raising the children.

- *Modified alternating weekends* (Friday night to Monday morning). This schedule has the advantage of allowing the noncustodial parent to drop the children off at school on Monday, as well as providing another night with the kids. Of particular importance in bitter divorces, it also presents less opportunity for conflict, as the custodial parent need not interact with the other parent when dropping the children off at school on Monday. If the noncustodial parent has some flexibility with regard to his or her work schedule, the transitions can become even smoother if the children are picked up directly from school on Friday.

- *Alternating weekends with a mid-week overnight.* (Friday night to Monday morning, and Wednesday night to Thursday morning). This clearly has the advantage of allowing the noncustodial parent more time with the children, but the schedule can be highly disruptive. Children in school are forced to consider whether it is Dad's night or Mom's night, and whether they have what they need at each residence. This type of arrangement can result in frequent trips back and forth between both parents' homes. (As in, "Mom, I forgot my math textbook at Dad's, and I have a test tomorrow." Or, "I accidentally brought the wrong clothes for school tomorrow. I need to go home and get something else.") While this schedule can work, it takes resilience on the part of the kids, who may never quite feel settled.

- *Alternating weekends, alternating or split holiday vacations, and part of the summer.* This option has the distinct advantage of allowing the noncustodial parent to spend extended amounts of time with the children when school is not in session. For instance, if the noncustodial parent can get the time off, arrange for day camp, daycare, or hire a part-time nanny, the children can spend several weeks in the summertime living with the noncustodial parent. Winter break can either be split (one week with each parent) or the children can alternate the time off (winter break with one parent one year, and the other parent the next year).

Of course, when the children are infants or toddlers, overnights at the noncustodial spouse's residence may not be appropriate. This is particularly true when the noncustodial parent never had sufficient time to bond with the children before the divorce. In these situations, the noncustodial parent may be stuck with short visits, at least until the children are older. There are many possibilities involving short visits. Here is one:

- *Three weekly visits of several hours each.* For exceptionally young children, being away from the parent with whom they are bonded can be quite uncomfortable. Limiting visits to a few hours at a time, at least initially, is a safe bet. For conflict-free parents, these visits can take place in the custodial parent's home, where the child will enjoy the security of familiar surroundings. For all others, either the noncustodial parent's home or a neutral location like a park (weather permitting) may be best. When the child becomes used to spending time alone with noncustodial parent, longer visits and overnights can be added.

Two Homes

Many divorcing spouses choose to have their children spend equal amounts of time with each parent. In this sense, the children truly do have two homes. This can be logistically or financially challenging, as the children will either need to cart their clothes and favorite belongings back and forth between two homes, or the children will need two sets of everything. In addition, parents who wish to share custody fairly equally and maintain two fully functional homes for their children must acknowledge that their children may frequently interact with the other parent's new partner. A few of the more common arrangements when the children live in two household are as follows:

- *One week on, one week off.* This has become a very common arrangement between spouses who live close together and both work. It has the obvious advantage of granting each parent equal time with the children, and the commensurate benefit of giving the children an equal chance to bond with both parents. This arrangement works particularly well when the parents are civil and can work together to raise the children with only minimal friction. In some situations the parents live close enough to one another that the children can walk or bike between houses. Many mental health professionals suggest that this schedule is most suitable for tweens and teens, as it involves spending seven days away from each parent.

151

- *One week on, one week off, with midweek dinner visit.* This schedule has the advantage of reducing the amount of time the child is away from each parent by including a weeknight dinner with the "off" parent. This often works well for young children who are uncomfortable being away from one or both parents for more than a few days at a time.

- *2-2-3.* This is an equal-time-sharing arrangement that merits a bit of explanation. Under this scenario, a two-week schedule is maintained. During Week 1, one parent has custody of the children from Monday morning to Wednesday morning, and again from Friday morning to Monday morning of Week 2. During Week 2, that same parent has custody of the children from Wednesday morning to Friday morning. In other words, Monday and Tuesday always go together, Wednesday and Thursday always go together, and the three-day weekend (Friday through Monday morning) always goes together. By rotating who takes custody of the children during each of these periods each week, the maximum amount of time that either parent will spend away from the children is the three-day weekend (hence the "3" in the 2-2-3). Here is a simple visual (Parent 1 is dark grey, Parent 2 is light grey):

Sun	Mon	Tue	Wed	Thu	Fri	Sat
1	2	3	4	5	6	7
8	9	10	11	12	13	14

The advantage of the 2-2-3 is simply that it limits time away from the children. The disadvantage is also clear – rotating weekdays as set forth above creates an additional transition and requires calendaring.

- *5-5-2-2.* A 5-5-2-2 is similar to a 2-2-3 in many respects. However, instead of alternating who takes custody of the children from Monday morning to Wednesday morning and from Wednesday morning to Friday morning, the Monday through Thursday schedule remains constant. In other words, one parent always has custody of the children on Monday and Tuesday, and the other parent always has custody of the children on Wednesday and Thursday. Three-day weekends are alternated in the same manner as the 2-2-3. Again, here is a simple visual (Parent 1 is dark grey, Parent 2 is light grey):

Sun	Mon	Tue	Wed	Thu	Fri	Sat
1	2	3	4	5	6	7
8	9	10	11	12	13	14

The advantage of the 5-5-2-2 is that the maximum amount of time either parent spends away from the children is five days (as opposed to seven with a "one week on, one week off" schedule). Another advantage of the 5-5-2-2 is that the Monday through Thursday schedule is consistent, which simply means that there are fewer transitions than with a 2-2-3.

- *Sunday, Monday, and Tuesday (all day) and Wednesday (morning) with one parent.* This is a compressed equal-time-sharing schedule, which has the advantage of decreasing the time between homes. However, this schedule has a significant disadvantage, which involves the increased chaos of moving every three and a half days. This also has the disadvantage of saddling one parent with the "less fun" beginning of the week, while the other parent gets to share the excitement of the weekend with the children.

- *Weekdays with one parent, weekends with another.* This presents a degree of stability and predictability that is nice, but the parent with weekday parenting duties may miss having time with the children while they are out of school. Furthermore, the parent who has the kids every weekend may long for a break.

- *Weekdays with one parent, weekends with another (modified in summer).* This modified schedule reverses itself in the summertime, so that the parent who has the children during the week during the school year has the children every weekend during the summer. This can provide a nice change of pace for both the parents and the children.

Someone Else's Home

Although ideally the children will live with one or both parents, in some cases this just isn't feasible. It could be that the parents are struggling financially or grappling with addiction. Regardless of the reason, if this applies to you, please make sure that you carefully specify exactly how the custodial arrangement will work. When will you see the children? Will you visit with them at their new home (the grandparents' residence, for instance)? How will you determine when you are ready to take the children back?

One Home Shared by Both Parents

This is a rather unconventional custody arrangement, but it can work in certain limited circumstances. If the children are extremely young *and* the parents get along beautifully, the house can be shared. While one parent is living with the children, the other lives in an apartment or makes other housing arrangements. The children enjoy the benefit that comes from the stability of having one home, but the parents may have a very hard time effectively living in two residences. The complication of continuing to share space with a former spouse also makes this a tricky arrangement. In short, though this arrangement is seldom advisable, it is worth mentioning.

Commuter Parents

Although it is always unfortunate, life circumstances sometimes require one parent to live in an entirely different state, or even on the opposite side of the country. For these noncustodial parents, flying out to see their children may be the only viable option when it comes to regular visits. Crossing the country every weekend is rarely an option, as the schedule will quickly wear the non-custodial parent down so much that it impacts his or her ability to function properly as a parent. For some truly hardy souls (who also can afford the significant expense of crossing the country so frequently), flying out to see the children every other weekend is a possibility. Again, depending on their work schedule, many parents find this arrangement is simply untenable.

At a minimum, a parent who lives on the opposite coast would be well advised to try to make the trip to the custodial parent's home at least once a month. If the relationship between the parents is anything but perfectly civil, the noncustodial parent may find that he or she has to book a hotel room for the weekend, essentially taking the kids on an extended sleepover once a month. This can be exciting for the children, but it also strips any sense of normalcy and permanency from the noncustodial parent's visits. If the custodial parent can tolerate sharing the family home with the visiting parent for a single weekend once a month, the kids benefit by enjoying the company of the visiting parent in familiar surroundings. This can be particularly important for very young children.

When the children are old enough to spend extended amounts of time away from the custodial parent, summer vacation becomes a golden opportunity for the noncustodial parent. Visits of several consecutive weeks can be arranged, allowing ample time for parent-child bonding. In addition, on occasion the children may enjoy the adventure of flying out to see the noncustodial parent for a long weekend.

Being a long-distance parent, while always challenging, has been aided greatly by technological innovation over the last two decades. Webcams and services such as Skype that offer video conferencing over the Internet can be hugely valuable to parents who need to stay in touch over great distances. Children often have a hard time with the telephone—particularly toddlers and pre-Ks. A voice alone simply isn't enough to entertain most children for an extended period of time. They simply need more stimulation. Cue the webcam.

The webcam and video-over-Internet is such a powerful tool for long-distance parents that some judges have ordered that the custodial parent make such tools available to the non-custodial parent. Reading bedtime stories, watching the children play or dance, expressing your delight when they show you a new treasure: these are all priceless interactions that were previously out of reach.

The lesson here: if you are an out-of-town parent, take advantage of every opportunity to interact with your children in this manner.

Because Internet video calls take some effort to arrange, parents should consider adopting a regular schedule for connecting with the kids. This has the added benefit of getting the children accustomed to regular interactions over the computer. Instead of complaining that they want to be outside playing or watching their favorite show, the kids will know that the time is always reserved for their out-of-town parent. As with everything else in an effective custodial relationship, communication and cooperation are critical.

2) Healthcare

Once you've determined where your children will live, you should consider how the location will impact their access to healthcare. For parents who live in the same town, the simplest solution is often to keep the same healthcare provider that the children used before the divorce. However, if one parent lives far enough away that visiting the children's physician becomes a hassle, alternate healthcare arrangements need to be made. With portable insurance, such as Anthem Blue Cross, simply finding the child a new primary care physician in the move-away parent's new hometown is an easy option. However, when one spouse receives employer-subsidized medical care through an HMO tied to a geographic area (such as Kaiser Permanente), arranging coverage for the children can be trickier. Some HMOs allow members to arrange for medical services for their children with other providers while they are outside of a specified geographic area, but this isn't always the case. On occasion, buying a portable policy for the children that can be used where both parents live is the best option available.

In addition to thinking about how medical coverage will be handled, you need to decide who will have the authority to handle certain medical matters, such as immunizations. Routine care typically doesn't require the consent of the other parent, but immunizations require coordination to avoid duplication. Most parents opt to require the consent of the other spouse before non-emergency surgery or hospitalization. Likewise, in all cases parents need to coordinate carefully when it comes to agreeing to and administering the children's medications.

3) Education

Although most parents agree that they want their children to enjoy a "good" education, many parents have strikingly divergent views about what exactly "good" means. To some, if means attending the same parochial school they attended as children. To others, it means doing whatever is necessary to get their children into a particular magnet school. For others still, it means doing all the heavy lifting themselves and home schooling their children. As with every aspect of a divorce, clear communication regarding desires and concerns is the key to coming to a workable compromise. Several factors should be analyzed before you decide how to educate children after divorce:

- *What can you afford?* Many divorcing couples whose children attend expensive private schools are deeply disappointed to discover that paying tens of thousands of dollars a year in private school tuition is no longer a viable option following divorce. Remember, each dollar after a divorce has to be stretched further, as each parent has to maintain a separate household. In many cases, something has to give. If it comes down to an annual extravagant vacation or private tuition, the choice is an easy one. However, some parents are already operating on a budget that allows for nothing more than necessities, and the luxury of private school simply isn't realistic any longer.

To make a sensible decision about what you can afford, do some detailed budgeting and be honest with yourself. "I'll figure out how to make it work" may be a commendable notion, but amassing large amounts of debt to send your children to private primary or secondary school is rarely sensible. If you are going to sink yourself into debt for your children, focus on college expenses instead. Although this can be extremely difficult to arrange, some enterprising parents manage to obtain scholarships for their children— the best possible outcome.

- *Where will they get the best education?* This is a highly subjective question, but one that some parents strangely fail to consider. Simply because they attended a private school decades ago, they assume that no better education exists. Do your research. If you have been sending your children to private school, you may be surprised to learn that the public high schools actually offer more honors and advanced placement courses than the local private school. In addition, you may have underestimated the resources available at public schools to deal with your children's individual needs.

- *What do your children want?* Of course, the heartbreaking reality may be that your children have been in private school for ten years, and the thought of leaving their friends behind and starting over at a public school is terrifying. In that case, you will undoubtedly do everything in your power to ensure that your children are able to finish secondary school with their core group of friends. On the other hand, some parents never ask their children what they want. They assume that they have to send their children to an expensive private school when the other kids in the neighborhood are all destined for the public school system. In that case the parents can expect that given a choice, their children will opt for public school.

- *Which school best reflects your core values?* This question is particularly applicable to parents with strong religious convictions. When both parents share the same faith and desires, sending the children to a religious school may be an easy choice. However, many divorced parents consist of a religious spouse and a non-religious spouse. This can create quite a bit of conflict when it comes to education. For instance, one parent may feel strongly that parochial school is the only reasonable choice for the children, while the other parent may feel that the public school system offers a broader and more competitive education.

  If you and your spouse disagree about whether your children should attend a religious school, try hard to understand exactly why your spouse feels the way that he or she does. Does his or her position stem from the fear that you won't instill any sense of religious tradition in the children? Or perhaps the opposite—that you will use religious education to indoctrinate the children in a worldview that sits in direct conflict with his or her own beliefs? Sometimes a compromise is possible. For instance, a couple that includes one Jewish parent might agree that the children will attend public school, but also agree that the children will all attend as much Hebrew School as necessary to celebrate their Bar or Bat Mitzvahs.

Aside from simply deciding where your children will attend school, a number of other details require your attention. For instance:

- *Who will participate in school activities?* If you wind up following the advice in this book and resolving your divorce with minimal tension, it is very likely that you and the child's other parent can both attend school functions. In fact, the joint show of support will be incredibly beneficial to your child's emotional health. Unfortunately, reality intrudes, and some parents simply don't want to share the same space with the other parent. In those cases, the parents should try to reach agreement on who will attend school functions that require a chaperone (i.e., trips to a museum) and who will help out in the classroom. The same principle applies to parent-teacher conferences. Figure out who will attend these important conferences now to avoid future conflict.

- *Will you reward good grades?* Consistent treatment with regard to grades is important, and if you hope to incentivize good grades with a reward system, you need to discuss this with your child's other parent.

- *Music lessons, after-school sports, and other extracurricular activities.* For many children, school doesn't end with the ringing of the bell. Music lessons, sports teams, drama rehearsal—the list goes on. Ideally, you will both be able to attend recitals, games, etc., but if that's not a possibility, try to come up with a schedule that allows equal participation in these important events. Also, discussing who will pay for lessons and fee-based programs is an important part of the divorce process for parents.

4) Holidays

For divorced parents, no time of the year is more difficult to manage than the holidays. Both parents typically want the children at their own home during the holidays. Conversely, neither parent wants to spend the holidays alone. To ensure that the children have the opportunity to spend with both parents, one of the following approaches can be used:

- *Alternating holidays*: This is a common way to ensure that both parents and the children get to enjoy the holidays together at least every two years without interruption. To further soften the absence of the children during the holidays, parents can stagger major holidays such as Thanksgiving and Christmas, for example. One parent can take the children for Thanksgiving, while the other has the children for Christmas. The following year the schedule can be reversed.

- *Dividing holidays in half.* This has the obvious advantage of ensuring that neither parent misses out on any particular holiday, but it has the serious disadvantage of making the holidays a little chaotic. This arrangement works particularly well if both parents live close to each other.

- *Celebrate twice:* Put yourself in your children's shoes. Wouldn't it be fabulous to celebrate major holidays twice? One parent can celebrate a holiday a week before its actual date, and the other can celebrate on the day itself. This works if one parent doesn't feel "cheated" by missing out on the real thing, and the travel plans of extended family aren't interrupted.

5) Decision Making

Many divorced parents struggle with the process of making decisions that affect their children. Who gets to decide important issues? Both parents jointly? The custodial parent? Another adult? In an ideal world, all parents would be able to reach agreement after carefully considering all available options, weighing each other's opinions fairly, and analyzing the needs of the children. While this is achievable, creating a little structure around the process of making decisions is often a good idea.

Be specific about who gets to make what type of decision, and when. For instance, like most parents, you may agree that everyday decisions affecting the children's lives will be made by the parent with whom the children are currently living. However, you may also agree that significant decisions (i.e., anything relating to healthcare or education) must be made by consensus.

In cases where one parent has sole physical custody and the other parent sees the children infrequently, it may make sense for the parent with physical custody to have broad discretion regarding the vast majority of decisions that impact the children's lives. In high conflict divorces with parents who struggle to come to any type of consensus regarding important decisions that impact the children, appointing a third party to make important decisions may be appropriate. However, that option should be reserved for only the most conflict-ridden parents. Appointing someone else as your child's guardian has serious consequences that should be discussed in detail with a family law attorney.

6) Dispute Resolution

Expect to reach an impasse with your children's other parent at least a few times over the years. It's inevitable. It may be something as seemingly innocuous as whether your children can attend the school trip to Washington D.C., or it may be as serious as whether or not a certain surgical procedure is appropriate. Regardless of the severity of the issue that is the subject of disagreement, you should agree on the approach you will take when the two of you just can't settle on a decision. The following are some of the standard approaches that parents use to settle disagreements. Consider each approach and think about how it might work given the dynamic between you and your children's other parent.

- *Mediation*: While mediation is addressed at length elsewhere in this book, it's worth mentioning again. Using a mediator is an excellent way to ensure that you are communicating clearly with the other parent while retaining complete control over the proceedings. You don't run the risk of putting important decisions in the hands of a third party, but you reap the benefit of professional guidance and support.

- *Consulting a Counselor or Therapist:* Sometimes simply obtaining the input of someone who is trained to diffuse tension, foster communication and facilitate cooperation is all that is needed to resolve conflict. Perhaps you simply can't understand why your children's other parent has taken such a hard line on a particular issue. A therapist may be able to coax an explanation from him or her. Understanding the underlying source of conflict often results in resolution. Quite often parents aren't really certain why they are arguing. It may not be the issue that is being argued about that is the problem, but a longstanding grievance that was never addressed. Therapists are quite skilled at uncovering sources of tension that make cooperation difficult.

- *Granting Authority to the Primary Caretaker:* As noted above, sometimes it simply makes sense to grant the primary caretaker the authority to make decisions when both parents can't agree. Certainly if one parent sees the children infrequently, his or her opinion should still be respected, but many parents agree that decision-making authority comes with the huge responsibility of being the children's primary caretaker.

- *Starting Slowly:* If two parents are having a particularly hard time agreeing on issues involving the children, it often makes sense to table large items for several months (if possible) while working on communication skills. By starting with basic questions, such as who will attend the children's recital, you may be able to rebuild enough trust to address larger issues. If needed, take baby steps.

7) Dealing with Moves

Nothing scares a parent more than the thought of watching helplessly as their children are moved away. The legal framework surrounding "move away" situations is explored in detail in the next section. The practical issues surrounding parental moves are many, and deserve some discussion. Consider the impact that a move may have on the children:

- *Less time with one parent.* If a parent with majority physical custody moves away and the other parent doesn't follow, it is likely that the children will see the other parent much less frequently. This is a huge source of stress for children who are bonded with the parent who isn't moving. Certain technological resources (i.e., online video chats) can lessen the shock, but they are no substitute for physical contact.

- *Loss or interruption of friendships.* For children who have lived most of their lives in the same neighborhood, a move can be socially devastating. Friends who have been around for years are suddenly out of reach, and the children will have to work hard to make new friends in an unfamiliar neighborhood. This can be difficult when the kids in a new neighborhood have already developed exclusive cliques.

- *Adjusting to a new school.* Each school has its own distinct feel, and relocating to a new one can truly rattle children. This is particularly true if children are forced to move mid-year. Teachers move at different paces, and being thrust into a new classroom is intimidating at best, and crippling at worst. Children may end up overwhelmed by the academic pace at the new school, or bored and restless and eager for distraction. Either way, adjustment is a challenge.

Moving the children is a surefire way to generate conflict. Avoiding a move during the already unsettling divorce process is ideal, but unfortunately it isn't always possible. Sometimes a parent must relocate because of a job. Or perhaps a parent who is overwhelmed may want to relocate to be closer to his or her own parents. Regardless of the reason, both parents need to think through the consequences of moving. In many cases, child support will need to be recalculated. In what feels like a stinging wound to the parent who stays behind, not only will child support payments increase (because the parent who stays behind will have the children less frequently), but he or she will also have to travel to see the kids.

If you are considering moving, show your children's other parent the respect of giving him or her as much notice as possible. Whatever you do, don't move without warning the other parent beforehand. It could jeopardize your custody of the children. Moving away from the area where the children have been living always presents a number of obstacles. Do everything you can to facilitate the transition, starting with clear and honest communication.

8) *Information Exchange*

Scheduling visits and arranging drop-offs are only a small element of a successful co-parenting relationship. It is critical for parents to keep adult affairs out of the communication loop with the children. For instance, a spouse who still harbors deep resentment over past infidelity must be certain this resentment doesn't infect communications with the children. Your kids should never be conduits for your personal motives. Don't use your kids to "spy" on the other parent, and certainly don't use them as messengers. If you want to know if your significant other is seeing someone else, ask him or her. Nothing puts children in a more awkward position than being forced to take sides and provide "intelligence" on the life of the other parent.

Never put a child in the position of asking for a child support payment, or for help with a medical bill. It is incredibly demoralizing for the child. Delivering a message to the other parent that the child knows is based on an unwelcome "adult" topic is awful. Child support is an adult issue. Parents must find a way to communicate about such issues without involving the kids. Failure to do so can be devastating for children for years to come. Divorcing can be unsettling and isolating, and depending on the age of your kids, you may be tempted to use them as a sounding board regarding family finances. Teaching kids financial responsibility at a young age is a great concept. Just don't let this notion cross over into discussions about support payments.

Some parents have an extremely hard time communicating with each other both during the divorce process and for years afterwards. Facing a spouse who may have deeply hurt you is difficult. Couples without children are often able to make a clean break and heal on their own. Those with kids, however, are not so lucky. Communication is critical, and the only matter for consideration is exactly how those information exchanges occur. Many therapists recommend that the parents transform their relationship from a deeply personal one to a business relationship. For some parents, this is easier said than done.

If you feel queasy at the thought of communicating with your child's other parent, you need to master the art of concise, business-like information exchanges. What exactly do you need to know? What do you need to communicate with the other parent? Think about this ahead of time. What homework still needs to be done? How are your children progressing with extra-curricular activities? Are there any disciplinary issues that need to be addressed? What are the kids doing for fun? Do you need to discuss any changes to the ground rules (see below)?

If you can't bear the thought of communicating in person with your child's other parent, consider exchanging information over the phone. If that is too hard, try email (or if you absolutely must) text messaging. In some instances, an uncooperative pair of parents needs to establish separate relationships with key individuals in the children's lives, such as doctors, teachers, nannies and event coordinators. Many such individuals don't want to communicate separately with each parent. Indeed, it creates quite a bit of extra work for them, so it is easy to understand their frustration. Nevertheless, until things calm down enough that jointly communicating with these individuals is possible, be firm in insisting on the necessity of separate meetings and information exchanges.

9) Consistency and Ground Rules

Children are remarkably adaptable. As a result, they are able to accommodate a certain degree of disparity when it comes to living in each parent's home. That said, when one parent is extremely heavy-handed with discipline, rules, and order, and the other parent subscribes to a less rigorous lifestyle for the kids, challenges can arise. It is hard enough for many married couples to settle on a set of rules with regard to raising their children together. Add divorce to the mix, and it becomes truly challenging.

The first step to achieving some minimum degree of consistency between two households is to establish an open flow of information. Highlight any behavioral issues you have noticed with your children and discuss how you would like to address them. To establish a better relationship with the children's other parent and minimize conflict, acknowledge your different parenting styles.

The next step to achieving a degree of consistency is to set a few ground rules. There is almost no chance that you and the children's other parent will agree on everything. Regardless of the particulars, parents who employ greatly differing parenting styles need to work together to establish some basic ground rules for their shared custodial relationship. For example, decide that no matter whose house the children are living in, they won't watch more than one hour of television a day. Or perhaps you can establish a ground rule based on consumption of fast food—not more than once a week.

Imagine the following scenario, and you will immediately grasp the problems that accompany the combination of vastly differing parenting styles and no ground rules:

Jan and Jeff have two children, Steve, aged 12, and Alice, aged 6. Jan is a very permissive parent. She thinks the kids should be able to dress however they like, listen to whatever strikes their fancy, and watch any sort of movie or play virtually any type of computer game. So long as the kids are in bed by midnight, she is also not particularly worried about their schedules. She thinks Steve should find the motivation for homework "from within" and she only wants Alice to learn a musical instrument "if she wants to." She does encourage Steve to continue pursuing his love of the electric guitar by taking him to lessons. Lastly, she has no problem with allowing the kids to subsist on a diet that largely consists of fast food and pizza.

Jeff is a very different type of parent altogether. When the kids spend the week at his house, they eat three healthy meals a day, are firmly tucked in bed by 8:30 pm (Alice) and 10:00 pm (Steve), watch no television, and study classical music with their father. Jeff refuses to support Steve's electric guitar lessons, insisting that if he wants to learn to play the guitar, he should start with classical guitar. While to many grownups Jeff seems like a good but somewhat severe parent, imagine how Steve and Alice feel about his parenting style. Able to run wild in Jan's home, Steve and Alice have naturally dubbed their father the "no fun" parent. Worse still, it takes the kids at least two days to resettle after the madness of living in Jan's house before they can transition into the lifestyle that prevails at Jeff's house. In short, the kids are continually off-balance because of their two drastically different lifestyles, and Jeff is constantly faced with the grumbling and unpleasant attitudes that result from his status as the less permissive parent.

As you might imagine, Jeff and Jan don't communicate well. They enjoy very different lifestyles, and their children pay the price for their unwillingness to lay down some fundamental "ground rules." Though it may seem that Jan should simply try to adhere to Jeff's more stringent parenting rules, this isn't necessarily the case. If Jan is going to impose any sort of discipline in the children's lives, it will only be if Jeff is willing to make a concession or two and loosen up a little. Jeff might consider an occasional trip to the pizza parlor, or perhaps letting the kids stay up late on an odd Friday night. And while Jeff detests television, he may consider letting the kids watch a few educational programs.

In the end, simply by conceding the electric guitar lessons, a slightly later bedtime, and loosening up on television, Jeff is able to get Jan to agree to the following ground rules:

- No more than four fast-food meals a week

- Homework will be done every night

- Piano lessons for Alice once a week, whether she likes it or not

- Electric guitar lessons for Jeff once a week

- No more than two hours of television a day

- Weekday bedtimes of 9:00 pm (Alice) and 10:30 pm (Steve)

The overriding purpose of ground rules is consistency. Leading two very different lifestyles is difficult for children. Remember, the ground rules are not only for your sanity, but also for your kids' well-being. You both want your children to do well. Laying down consistent rules will not only enable them to perform better in school and other activities, but it will also prevent one parent from being put in the unfair position of being the sole disciplinarian. Some topics for consideration as ground rules:

- Sleep schedules (i.e., when is bedtime?)

- Disciplinary styles ("time-outs" vs. "extra chores" etc.)

- Music lessons and sports (mandatory vs. discretionary)

- Allowance (i.e., how much?)

- Policies on driving (for teenagers over 16)

- Sleepovers with friends (permitted, and if so, how often?)

- Television watching (what shows and how often?)

- Computer games (what type and when can they be played?)

- Diet and nutrition (types of foods, permissible splurges)

- Religious education (what type and how much?)

Other Issues to Consider

Hired Help – Nannies and Other Caretakers

Though the term is a bit outdated, please note that in this discussion the term "nanny" is simply meant to refer to a caretaker for the children, whether male or female. If you are fortunate enough to have the financial resources available to hire a nanny in lieu of other arrangements (such as daycare), you may find that your nanny provides a welcome dose of stability to the lives of your children. Indeed, when everything else seems to be coming apart, kids subject to joint-physical custody will be greatly relieved to know that the nanny will travel with them between homes.

Don't surprise your nanny with the news of divorce at the last minute. Let him or her know that you are contemplating separation, and that your children may soon be splitting time between two households. Also try to get a sense of whether he or she plans to stick around for the next year or so, and if your kids have already bonded with the nanny over a period of months or years, encourage him or her to stick it out, at least for the time being. Let your nanny know that the divorce process will be highly unsettling for your children, and that he or she provides an invaluable sense of stability. If needed, you might even consider offering your nanny a raise to ensure his or her continued service.

Ideally, you and your spouse will sit down with the nanny together and explain your new custody arrangement. Explain that the fundamental ground rules that the nanny has been operating under haven't changed, but that he or she will be expected to travel back and forth between two homes. You should also address compensation (who will be responsible for paying the nanny, and when). Lastly, without asking your nanny to divulge information provided to him or her in confidence by the children, do ask for regular updates regarding the nanny's sense of the children's well being. Divorce can make children act out, and in many cases a nanny will witness the most severe manifestations of this phenomenon. Your nanny will be of invaluable service when it comes to assessing the need for therapy or a simple "heart-to-heart" with your children.

The New Partner

Nothing can be more traumatic for a divorced parent than being introduced to the other parent's new partner. Entire books have been written about the art of step parenting and the art of interacting with stepparents. First, chant the mantra over and over again in your head, "I will act like a grownup for the sake of my children." It is incredibly common (and very destructive) for one parent to demonize the other parent's new partner or spouse. Of course, this is particularly true when the new spouse was embroiled in an affair with the parent prior to divorce. Anger and resentment are natural, and in many cases, simply inevitable. If you find yourself seething over the very existence of the "home-wrecking" lover who is now the other parent's new spouse, you are not alone. Talk it out in therapy, shout your frustrations into the wind, or otherwise deal with your anger and disappointment. Do not drag your children into your emotional minefield.

In some cases, one parent may actually take a liking to the other parent's new spouse. This is becoming more common as the stigma surrounding divorce and remarriage fades, and spouses increasingly turn to conflict resolution (e.g., mediation) to resolve disagreements during the divorce process. If you are lucky enough to find yourself charmed by the new addition to the family, the process of integrating the kids' new stepparent into the custody routine is fairly simple. You likely won't mind if the stepparent attends important events in your children's lives (recitals, graduations, etc.), and you won't flinch if the stepparent is the sole caretaker of your children for periods of time (for instance, if the children's other parent travels frequently for work).

In other cases, one parent simply can't stand the other parent's new partner. This can obviously make interaction between the two tense at best, and can make discussions regarding the role of the new stepparent very difficult. If you find yourself livid at the very thought of the new stepparent interacting with your children, you have your work cut out for you. Remember, you can't tell your children's other parent whom to choose as a partner. It's simply not your decision. Sooner or later, you will have to learn to cope as best you can. While it may be wise to avoid face-to-face interactions with the new stepparent, be prepared to encounter him or her on the phone on occasion despite the most diligent avoidance strategy.

Regardless of whether you are pleased with the other parent's choice of a partner or not, you will have to address certain issues. Some basic items for discussion include the following:

- *What will the children call the stepparent?* This is a very sensitive topic for many parents. Fear of being displaced is a very powerful emotion, and the possibility that the children will call this new stepparent "dad" or "mom" is extremely threatening. Therapists profess differing opinions when it comes to the appropriateness of calling a stepparent "mom" or "dad." Some believe it is patently unfair to the true parent, while others state that using those terms is simply natural for children in some custodial situations. As always, coming to a clear understanding with the children's other parent is critical. Having your children continually refer to their stepparent as "mom" or "dad" can be devastating when this was never discussed beforehand.

If either you or your spouse are particularly sensitive about the possibility of having your children call someone else "mom" or "dad," you should both strongly consider honoring the other's feelings. Come up with another name. In many cases, simply having the children refer to the stepparent by his or her first name is appropriate. If this doesn't feel right, get creative. Just do something that allows the concerned parent to hang on to his or her treasured title.

- *How will the stepparent handle discipline?* Nothing is a surer recipe for an extensive custody dispute than the children's insistence that the stepparent is engaging in unduly severe discipline. No parent wants to think of any adult treating his or her children harshly. Indeed, even teachers are often censured for the most rudimentary discipline. Imagine the emotional response when a parent discovers that a detested stepparent spanked one of the kids. It gets ugly. Avoid this scenario by discussing discipline ahead of time.

Before insisting that the new stepparent play no role in disciplining your child, think about how this might be damaging. Indeed, making the stepparent a "toothless" adult figure in the children's lives rarely does anyone any good. If the stepparent can't govern through discipline, he or she may be forced to provide inducements for good behavior. This can lead to very spoiled children. Imagine if providing a chocolate chip cookie was the only way to get your children to behave? It would be disastrous, wouldn't it?

Discuss discipline with the child's other parent. Try to agree upon appropriate methods of discipline that can be used by the stepparent (time-outs, restricting access to favorite activities, etc.). Above all, be *clear*. If you are spooked about the thought of anyone else disciplining your child, express your concerns to the children's other parent as gently as you can. You may be surprised by his or her ability to reassure you.

The Legal Framework for Custody

How Does a Judge Decide on Custody?

Because awarding custody is arguably the most important decision that a family court makes in a divorce, and because most judges will freely admit that they haven't obtained the training or education required to effectively determine who should bear primary responsibility for raising a child, a court will invariably rely heavily on the recommendations of various experts. These experts play a critical role in the state-mandated mediation that must occur before a judge makes a decision regarding custody. The experts, and the judges who turn the experts' opinions into binding orders, rely on several factors when making custody decisions, but first and foremost among them is the degree to which a child is bonded with each parent.

Is a Child's Choice of Parent Influential?

Forcing a teenager to live with a particular parent against his or her will is problematic, and can clearly cause a great deal of conflict. Judges are aware of this, and in California they are required to give the child's choice "due weight." Exactly what this means is subject to the interpretation of each judge. Typically, the child's preference will be considered as appropriate based on the child's intelligence, maturity, and motivation for the choice. In other words, the judge can essentially do whatever he or she likes.

Some judges will meet privately with children as young as eight years old, while others prefer to rely exclusively on the advice of custody evaluators. If they choose to meet with children privately, note that experienced judges are quick to spot cases of parental coaching. Some parents will endlessly rehearse the appropriate answers to questions before the children meet with the judge. This is easier to spot than most parents realize.

Sometimes an older child will come forward and ask to speak to a judge privately. Most judges will honor this request. If nothing else, a kindly judge may explain to the child why he or she couldn't honor the child's request. Children want to be heard, and acknowledgment from the judge that their request didn't fall on deaf ears can be emotionally helpful. One important note of caution, however. If you end up litigating (please don't) and your children meet privately with a judge, do not tell them that whatever they say to the judge will be kept confidential. If their statements are later revealed to the other parties, they will be devastated.

Custody Evaluators – Who Are They?

Nearly every court in California uses a system that appoints a mental health professional to conduct interviews and make custody recommendations to the court. The recommendations made by this expert are nearly always honored by the presiding judge. Therefore, it is the expert and not the judge who plays the most critical role in custody evaluations.

Custody evaluators come from a variety of backgrounds, ranging from licensed social workers to doctors of psychology. Depending on the county, an evaluator can be either a court employee or a professional in private practice who agrees to accept court referrals. The qualifications and skill set offered by each evaluator vary greatly, particularly among evaluators who accept court referrals.

Some are good, and some are bad. As with every other aspect of your divorce, you are much better off negotiating a workable custody arrangement directly with your spouse.

Attorneys for Children

Rarely, and only in certain counties, a judge will appoint a separate attorney to represent the interests of a child in a hotly contested divorce. The reasons vary, but typically the judge will do so if the attorney for one spouse insists on calling the child to the stand as a witness. The cost of hiring the attorney falls on the spouse who made the appointment necessary. If nothing else, the threat of paying an additional $10,000 in fees to the child's attorneys will often convince a spouse to back down from the controversial position. One of the dangers associated with granting a child his or her own attorney is a false sense of empowerment (i.e., the child's perception of his or her ability to control the outcome of a custody dispute will be overinflated). The other risk is simply that the judge simply won't place much weight on the input from the child's attorney.

Moving Children Away

As noted earlier in this chapter, perhaps nothing causes more angst to a noncustodial parent than the other parent's decision to move the children to a new geographic area, whether it is across the state or across the country. You have already read about the practical challenges that accompany relocation. This section simply explores the legal framework that surrounds such a move.

The law governing the custodial parent's ability to relocate with the children has changed repeatedly. Prior to 1991, in most instances the custodial parent was permitted to move the children wherever he or she wanted. To keep the children where they were, the noncustodial spouse had to show that the move would be detrimental to the child, something that is very difficult to prove.

In 1991 things changed with the California Appellate Court's decision in *In Re Marriage of Carlson*. In *Carlson*, the court stated that children can be moved only if doing so is in their best interests. This decision shifted the burden of proof entirely to the custodial parent. It is very difficult to demonstrate that moving away from the noncustodial parent somehow benefits the child. Under the reasoning of the court, the move away had to be necessary, not simply convenient.

In 1996 things changed yet again with the California Supreme Court's decision in *In Re Marriage of Burgess*. In *Burgess*, the court stated that a custodial parent doesn't need to prove that moving the children is beneficial. The burden of proof once again shifted to the noncustodial parent, who had to show that the move was so harmful to the children that an immediate change of custody was required to protect their welfare. The custodial parent who wished to relocate only had to show that the move was made in good faith (i.e., it wasn't intended solely to deprive the other parent of custody).

Burgess is currently the controlling law on the ability of custodial parents to move their children away. Custody evaluators may try to skirt *Burgess* simply because it does not give much, if any, weight to the children's desires when it comes to moving. Furthermore, *Burgess* is reviled by some because it limits the rights of the noncustodial parent, and places little importance on the stability derived from having two involved parents. Indeed, the core principle that can be derived from *Burgess* is that the custodial parent's bond with the child is of paramount importance. Right or wrong, *Burgess* is the reality that judges face when presiding over divorces and custody disputes.

Cases in which one parent wants to move the children to another geographic area are heavily litigated, simply because nothing strikes fear into the heart of noncustodial parents like the possibility of having to travel great distances to see their kids. A noncustodial parent will attempt to prove that the decision to move was made in bad faith, and the custodial parent is doing nothing more than punishing the noncustodial parent by depriving him or her of visitation rights. This can get quite ugly.

If you are a custodial parent who wants to move away with your children, make sure you do it right. You need to either obtain the written consent of the other parent or seek the court's permission to move. Failure to do either of these things might result in a court order requiring that you return your children to California until a hearing is held. Worse yet, a court might interpret your disappearance with the children as a case of child abduction, something that might jeopardize your status as the custodial parent.

CHAPTER 9

Estate Planning and Divorce

"Wills, Trusts, Powers of Attorney, and Survivor Benefits"

Amending or revoking the documents that determine how a couple's affairs will be handled upon death or incapacity is often overlooked during divorce. It is a mistake to neglect this important part of the divorce process, yet it happens all too often. You may be completely occupied with deciding how to divide your community property, calculate support payments, or work out a custody schedule. The chance that either of you will pass away in the meantime seems remote. Nevertheless, the case law in California is full of examples of how neglecting to plan properly before, during, and after a divorce can be catastrophic.

Here are some of the basic things you need to know about wills, trusts, powers of attorney, survivor benefits and divorce:

- Once your divorce is final, a court will automatically invalidate any bequest to your former spouse contained in your will.

- If you die during the divorce process and you haven't yet revoked your will, your soon-to-be former spouse will be entitled to everything you gave him or her in the will.

- A gift to your former spouse contained in a trust agreement is not automatically revoked upon divorce in all cases. To be certain, you should revoke the trust yourself.

- If you die during the divorce process and you haven't yet revoked your trust, your soon-to-be former spouse will receive everything he or she is entitled to according to the trust.

- You can freely revoke or amend any power of attorney or health care directive at any point during the divorce process.

- Some retirement plans are creatures of federal law. As a result, if you forget to change your beneficiary designation to list someone other than your former spouse after divorce, you may encounter trouble.

Estate Planning, Practically Speaking

<u>Wills</u>

Many divorcing couples simply have two wills, one for each spouse. As noted below, California courts have held that any provision providing for a former spouse in a will is automatically revoked upon divorce. In other words, if you name your spouse as your primary beneficiary upon your death and forget to revoke your will before divorce, a final divorce decree will automatically strip your spouse out of your estate plan. For most divorcing couples, this is good news, as there are other people each spouse would rather benefit.

However, if a spouse dies during the divorce proceedings, but before the divorce is final, problems arise. Imagine the following scenario: John and Sue Smith execute a will in 2000 naming each other as the sole beneficiary of their respective estates. In 2010 they begin the divorce process.

Though they are certain they want a divorce, they take their time untangling their affairs, and John dies unexpectedly later that year. Despite the natural implication that John wouldn't want all of his assets flowing to his soon-to-be-former spouse, that is exactly what happens. Simply revoking his old will and signing a new one would have taken care of the issue.

Revoking a will is permitted even after you've file a petition for dissolution, a summons has been served and an automatic restraining order is in place.

Note that if you want to leave something for your former spouse in your will, you need to explicitly state that you are intentionally providing for him or her. If you do not make such a statement, a court may decline to honor the portion of your will that benefits your spouse (see below).

<u>Living Trusts</u>

Although a divorce or annulment does revoke provisions for a former spouse in a will, it doesn't automatically revoke a living trust in every instance. If you and your spouse have established a living trust, your required course of action depends on where you stand in the overall divorce process.

- If you haven't yet filed a petition for dissolution, chances are you can revoke your family trust simply by delivering a signed statement to your spouse indicating that you are doing exactly that. In rare circumstances, a trust agreement will require that both spouses consent to revocation. Check your trust agreement to determine if this applies to you.

- If you've already filed a petition for dissolution and a summons has been served, an automatic restraining order comes into effect that prohibits you from modifying your trust or creating a new trust without the consent of your spouse or a court order. However, you are permitted to revoke your trust by filing and serving notice on your spouse before the change takes effect.

- Once your divorce is final, of course you are free to revoke your family trust and establish a trust of your own. Simply send a signed statement to your former spouse indicating your decision. Again, check your trust agreement to ensure that the consent of both of you isn't required for revocation (which is unusual).

Powers of Attorney and Health Care Directives

A divorce automatically revokes your appointment of a former spouse as your agent. However, you will certainly want to change your nomination for your primary agent under both your power of attorney and your health directive in the interval between separation and divorce. The Automatic Restraining Order that comes into effect when you file for divorce has no impact on your ability to amend either your power of attorney or your health care directive.

Retirement Plans

The manner in which a retirement plan is administered upon your death is governed by federal law if the underlying plan is also subject to federal law. In short, if dividing the retirement plan upon divorce requires a Qualified Domestic Relations Order (QDRO), and you forget to amend your beneficiary designation after divorce, federal law will control the disposition of that retirement plan upon your death (see page 67).

The Legal Framework for Estate Planning

Revocation of Provisions Relating to Former Spouse Upon Divorce

Section 6122 of the California Probate Code provides that unless a will expressly provides otherwise, the provisions of that will providing for the spouse and any nomination of the spouse as executor, trustee, conservator, or guardian are revoked upon divorce.

Be warned, however, that if you want to continue to provide for the children of your former spouse after divorce in your will or living trust, you should amend the document and specifically state your intention to do so. Several cases in California have held that provisions in a will executed before divorce that provided for a spouse's children from another relationship are deeded invalid upon divorce. If you intend to provide for your step-children even after divorce, you should amend your estate planning documents accordingly.

Revoking a Living Trust

Section 15401(a)(2) of the California Probate Code provides that in addition to any other method of revocation permitted by the trust agreement itself, a trust may be revoked by a signed writing delivered to the trustee during the lifetime of the person who created the trust. However, if the trust instrument specifies a particular method of revoking a trust and makes it the exclusive method of revoking the trust, the signed writing noted above may not have any effect. When in doubt, read your trust carefully to ensure that you won't be violating the terms of the trust by simply handing your spouse a signed letter stating your intent to revoke the trust.

Dividing Specialized Irrevocable Trusts

Some couples with large estates engage in sophisticated planning employing such mechanisms as charitable remainder trusts, life insurance trusts, and qualified personal residence trusts. Dividing these trusts requires specialized knowledge and should not be attempted without the counsel of an experienced trusts and estates attorney.

CHAPTER 10

Frequently Asked Questions

"There are no dumb questions... (in this book, anyway)"

What is the difference between mediation and arbitration?

Both mediation and arbitration are alternatives to litigation. However, in mediation you and your spouse make all of the critical decisions, while in arbitration a third party (often a retired judge or a seasoned attorney) makes the decisions for you. Much like litigation, arbitration puts control of the proceedings in someone else's hands. It is often preferable to litigation because it is typically more efficient and less expensive.

What if my mediator sides with my spouse?

Mediators are ethically bound to act impartially. Indeed, neutrality is the very lifeblood that sustains the profession. Although no single governing body controls the ethical standards that govern mediator behavior, both the Academy of Family Mediators and the Society or Professionals in Dispute Resolution (in connection with the American Bar Association and the American Arbitration Association) have adopted model standards for mediators. These standards include provisions about neutrality and impartiality.

Most importantly, simply try to get a feel for whether your mediator is treating you fairly. If you continually find yourself doubting your mediator's impartiality, you can either (1) bring it to his or her attention (which will almost always be well received and have a discernable effect), or (2) simply walk away and find a new mediator.

How much do mediators charge, and how do they bill for their time?

The way mediators bill for their time is almost as varied as their individual mediation styles. Some bill hourly and collect fees at the end of each session (much like a therapist), while others collect a substantial up-front retainer and simply draw down the retainer as hours accumulate. Other mediators charge a mixture of flat fees and an hourly rate. For instance, some mediators charge a flat fee for all of the paperwork involved in a divorce (including drafting the marital separation agreement, if they are an attorney), while charging an hourly fee for mediation sessions.

Hourly rates for mediation range widely depending on professional licensing and geographic location. The most expensive mediators will almost always be experienced attorneys in large metropolitan areas. Fees up to $500 an hour are not uncommon. The cheapest mediators will often be relatively new therapists or financial professionals, who may charge significantly less than attorneys. Fees as low as $150 an hour may be charged in less competitive markets. Do keep in mind that using a non-attorney mediator will almost always require hiring an attorney to do the work that the mediator isn't permitted to complete (such as drafting the marital separation agreement), though some non-attorney mediators charge their clients a flat fee for paperwork and then outsource the drafting of the marital separation agreement to an attorney, an arrangement that can work well in many instances.

Who pays for mediation?

This question is often a topic that comes up during the first mediation session. In short, you and your spouse can decide who should pay for the sessions. Some mediators will ask you and your spouse to sign an agreement stating that you are both responsible for mediator fees. If this is the case, and your spouse agrees to pay for mediation, you would be well advised to verify that the sessions are paid for in full so that you aren't left responsible for the bills if your spouse can't pay.

I want to get divorced but my spouse doesn't. Can mediation help?

Yes. However, to accomplish a peaceful divorce, your spouse will have to accept the reality of your situation. Getting your spouse to this place isn't always easy, but a mediator may be able to help. Have your spouse contact the mediator over the phone. The mediator may be able to convince your spouse to come in for an initial meeting, and then to commit to simply taking each session one at a time. You, your spouse, and the mediator can work together to evaluate the effectiveness of the sessions. Over time, your spouse may become more comfortable with the concept of living apart from you. A therapist may also prove extremely useful in helping your spouse adjust to the reality of his or her new life.

If after several sessions your spouse is still unwilling to discuss divorce, you may need to retain an attorney to file for divorce on your behalf. California is a no-fault state, and either spouse can unilaterally end a marriage. Unfortunately, your spouse's unwillingness to enter into constructive mediation sessions may signal that he or she is simply unwilling to let go, and that he or she will drag out the divorce proceedings as long as possible.

What if I want to tell the mediator something privately?

Private sessions with a mediator are called "caucuses." Some mediators use them judiciously, while others refuse to use them at all. Equality in caucusing is important to many mediators. In other words, if you meet separately with the mediator, your spouse should have the opportunity to do so as well.

It is important to set ground rules for caucusing before you begin. Will the sessions be confidential? In some mediations, what is discussed in caucuses may only be revealed by the participating spouse, not by the mediator. In other mediations nothing that is discussed separately is confidential with respect to the other spouse—i.e., everything may be revealed in joint sessions. Most mediators will leave the choice up to the clients.

Does this mean that you can't pick up the phone and simply have a private conversation with your mediator? Not at all. Most mediators do not object to an occasional phone call, and most do not insist on personally divulging information you revealed during the phone call to your spouse. Your mediator might encourage *you* to divulge this information, but that's typically the extent of it. Of course, if you reveal a piece of information to your mediator over the phone or during a private session that the mediator deems critical to fair negotiations, and you refuse to share this information with your spouse, the mediator may be forced to resign.

If I mediate do I have to go to court?

In California, the answer is no. Certainly there are exceptions, but in most cases the mediator will simply handle all of the court filings for you, and you need only sign the appropriate documents.

When is mediation inappropriate?

If you find yourself so crippled by depression or anger that you simply can't focus, you may want to delay mediation until you've had time to settle a bit. Mediators can handle a wide range of emotion during a mediation session, but if you are unable to be present and focused much of the time, you may want to put off mediation temporarily.

Mediation is never appropriate if you feel so threatened by your spouse that even the presence of a mediator does little to make you feel safe. If you are in an abusive relationship, or fear the physical retaliation of your spouse if you don't acquiesce to his or her demands, you should hire a divorce litigator.

What if I decide I don't want to get divorced after all?

If the change of heart is unilateral (i.e., your spouse still desires the divorce), you may still end up divorced against your will. However, if during mediation you and your spouse make amends and decide to work on your marriage, your mediator will be delighted. Mediators are peacemakers, and reconciliation is a pleasure to witness. If you find yourself in this happy situation, you can simply stop the divorce process.

I already have a lawyer, but I've heard that mediation is a better way to get divorced. Can I use a mediator too?

Absolutely. Mediators work with attorneys on a regular basis. However, it's important to gauge whether or not your attorney is mediation-friendly. On a rare occasion, an attorney simply doesn't understand or value the process. It may fly in the face of the attorney's business model, and he or she may resist bringing in a mediator. In most cases, though, lawyers are happy to work with mediators during the divorce process.

Keep in mind that while nearly all mediators actively advocate the use of one or more attorneys as independent reviewers of the final marital separation agreement, not all mediators are open to having attorneys participate in the sessions themselves. Having two litigators present while attempting to mediate can prove challenging and counterproductive, and having only a litigator present (representing one spouse) creates a harmful power imbalance.

I'd like to keep some of my financial information private. Do I have to reveal everything to my spouse during mediation?

The answer to this question is an emphatic *yes*, you do. Financial information is never confidential in divorce proceedings. Quite to the contrary, you are required to fully divulge any and all financial information to your spouse. Doing so is the only way to ensure a fair and durable marital separation agreement. Hiding information from your spouse, while not only counterproductive, can result in serious legal penalties. Indeed, any asset that you hide from your spouse will be awarded to him or her under California law. See page 53 for more information on the law behind this.

What if our joint tax returns are audited after our divorce? I never looked at the returns. My spouse handled everything.

The "innocent spouse rule" offers some degree of protection if you signed a joint return without knowledge of tax mistakes or misrepresentations made by your former spouse. Proving that you are an innocent spouse, however, is no small task. To qualify for the rule, you must meet the following criteria:

- You filed a joint return on which there was an understatement of tax due to an erroneous item relating to your spouse.

- You didn't know, and had no reason to know, about the understatement when you signed the return.

- Looking at all the facts and circumstances, it would be unfair to make you pay the tax.

- You apply for relief under this provision within two years after the IRS begins trying to collect the tax from you.

The lack of knowledge requirement is one of the biggest problems in obtaining innocent spouse relief. You will not receive any relief if you knew the return was incorrect (or even if the court thinks you *should have known*.) Some court decisions indicate that you can't satisfy this condition unless you actually examine the return and ask questions about anything that doesn't seem right— which most people consider an unrealistic expectation in many marriages. Other decisions seem to penalize a spouse for being well educated, suggesting that anyone with a good academic background should have identified the problems in the return. Regardless, proving innocence is possible, but be prepared for a battle.

While this may seem daunting, keep in mind that you can negotiate a clause in your marital separation agreement that states that your spouse will pay for any past due taxes, interest, and penalties. You can also specify a method of reimbursement if this happens to you, and so long as your spouse hasn't filed for bankruptcy, it should be fully enforceable. Note, however, that the IRS isn't bound by your agreement. If you can't prove that you qualify for the innocent spouse rules, the IRS can and will come after you for the tax due.

How do we split the tax refund we are expecting this year?

Simply put, you can negotiate its division as you would any other asset. If the refund is based on a joint tax return, you are both entitled to it.

Who gets to file head-of-household status after our divorce?

To qualify for head-of-household status, you must satisfy all of the following requirements:

- You must be unmarried at the end of the year or live apart from your spouse for more than six months;

- You must maintain a household for your child (even if you do not claim him or her as a dependent), or a dependent parent, or other qualifying dependent relative;

- The household must be your home and generally must also be the main home of the qualifying dependent (i.e. your children must live with you more than half the year);

- You must provide more than half the cost of maintaining the household; and

- You must be a U.S. citizen or resident alien for the entire tax year.

As indicated above, a taxpayer does not need to claim a dependency exemption to file as head of household. Therefore, if you have custody of the children more than half the year, you can still file for head of household regardless of whether you allocate (by completing IRS Form 8332) the dependency exemption to your ex-spouse.

Obtaining head of household tax filing status generally depends upon the custodial arrangement. If your marital separation agreement provides for joint physical custody, you might want to consider indicating which child lives with which parent for more than one half of the year. If you have two children, both you and your ex-spouse may be able to qualify for head of household status, so long as one of your children lives with you more than half of the year, and your other child lives with his or her other parent more than half of the year.

Note that if you qualify for head of household status, you may also qualify to benefit from any applicable "Dependent Care Credit" and/or "Earned Income Tax Credit."

I signed a prenuptial agreement before I got married. How will that affect my divorce settlement?

California courts generally honor premarital agreements unless evidence of fraud or unconscionability is presented. That said, if your circumstances have changed dramatically since you signed the agreement, you and your spouse may agree that the document is no longer particularly relevant and agree to mediate the issues that were previously covered by the prenuptial agreement. To come to this decision, though, it is vital that you seek the input of an attorney who represents *only you* first. This will ensure that you realize what you are giving up by mediating issues that are addressed in the agreement. Once you are comfortable that reopening these issues for discussion is desirable, a mediator will be able to help you and your spouse come to a new agreement.

Of course, a prenuptial agreement does not cover every aspect of a divorce. Indeed, a prenuptial can't address custody issues or child support. Regardless of the fact that your prenuptial agreement may address the subjects of property division and spousal support, you will benefit greatly from using a mediator to handle the issues that accompany divorce when children are involved.

My spouse and I live in separate states. Can we mediate our divorce?

If you and your spouse are separated and living in separate states, you can still mediate your divorce. However, you must first ensure that one of you meets the residency requirements for filing for divorce in a particular state. To file for divorce in California, one of the parties to the marriage must have been a resident of the state for six months and of the county in which the proceeding is filed for the three-month period ending upon filing.

Mediation works best in person—period. If the out-of-state spouse can fly into the state where mediation will occur for one or more intensive multi-day sessions, the expense of travel can be minimized. While this is the ideal approach, technology has made mediating using conferencing software possible. One spouse can meet with the mediator in person, while the other participates through video chat.

My spouse is a member of the military. What are the rules regarding the division of his/her pension?

Military divorces are subject to specific federal rules that supersede state law. Note, however, that the Uniformed Services Former Spouse Protection Act does not confer an entitlement to a portion of the retired pay to a former spouse as a result of the length of a marriage or number of years of service concurrent with a marriage. Instead, it simply permits a court to dispose of retirement pay for pay periods beginning after June 25, 1981. In California, the retirement pay is either disposed of as the service-member's separate property or as the couple's community property, depending on the circumstances.

Further, once a court has awarded a former spouse a portion of retired pay as property, the former spouse may apply to have his or her portion delivered directly from the government. To qualify for a direct payment, the law requires a former spouse to have been married to the member during at least 10 years of the member's service creditable for retired pay.

In short, if either you or your spouse is an active duty or retired member of the military, you should make sure that your mediator is familiar with the rules of the Uniformed Services Former Spouse Protection Act.

How are Social Security benefits handled in a divorce?

Your entitlement to Social Security benefits is determined entirely by federal law. The rules are fairly simple. If (1) you've been married at least 10 years, (2) you've been divorced for at least 2 years, (3) you're at least 62 years old, and (4) you are unmarried, you are eligible to collect benefits based on your ex spouses work record.

As a spouse, you can receive up to 50% of your husband's full Social Security benefit—or less if you take benefits before your full retirement age. In the alternative, you can receive benefits based on your own earnings history, if the number is higher. Note that your benefit does not reduce your ex-spouse's benefit in any way. In addition, your ex-spouse's decision to remarry (and his or her subsequent divorce, if applicable) won't have any effect on your benefit.

My spouse plans to file for bankruptcy. What can I do to protect myself, and how do we manage the timing of the process?

First of all, if your spouse's creditors won't force him or her into involuntary bankruptcy, it's typically best to obtain a divorce before filing for bankruptcy. The logic behind this is fairly straightforward. Spousal support and child support are not dischargeable in bankruptcy, but property obligations are dischargeable. To ensure that the bankruptcy court honors your decision to treat the distribution of various assets to you as spousal support (for instance), you should make sure your final marital separation agreement reflects this distinction. By completing your divorce before your spouse files for bankruptcy, you are greatly increasing the odds that your assets will be treated in the manner you desire (and thereby sheltered from creditors).

Note also that if you file for bankruptcy before the divorce, the Bankruptcy Court must approve any agreements involving property or debts before the matter goes to the family court. This is a headache, to say the least, and it can result in the rejection of your financial arrangements as noted above.

It is in your interest to settle and complete all property division before (or at) the time of divorce, simply to avoid having creditors claim the property at a later date. Be sure to consult with a bankruptcy attorney, however, to ensure that you aren't engaging in what could be considered a fraudulent transfer.

Appendix

California Family Code Sections

Exhibit A – Custody

Family Code § 3002. "Joint custody" means joint physical custody and joint legal custody.

Family Code § 3003. "Joint legal custody" means that both parents shall share the right and the responsibility to make the decisions relating to the health, education, and welfare of a child.

Family Code § 3004. "Joint physical custody" means that each of the parents shall have significant periods of physical custody. Joint physical custody shall be shared by the parents in such a way so as to assure a child of frequent and continuing contact with both parents, subject to Sections 3011 and 3020.

Family Code § 3006. "Sole legal custody" means that one parent shall have the right and the responsibility to make the decisions relating to the health, education, and welfare of a child.

Family Code § 3007. "Sole physical custody" means that a child shall reside with and be under the supervision of one parent, subject to the power of the court to order visitation.

Family Code § 3011. In making a determination of the best interest of the child in a proceeding described in Section 3021, the court shall, among any other factors it finds relevant, consider all of the following:

(a) The health, safety, and welfare of the child.

(b) Any history of abuse by one parent or any other person seeking custody against any of the following:

(1) Any child to whom he or she is related by blood or affinity or with whom he or she has had a caretaking relationship, no matter how temporary.

(2) The other parent.

(3) A parent, current spouse, or cohabitant, of the parent or person seeking custody, or a person with whom the parent or person seeking custody has a dating or engagement relationship. As a prerequisite to the consideration of allegations of abuse, the court may require substantial independent corroboration, including, but not limited to, written reports by law enforcement agencies, child protective services or other social welfare agencies, courts, medical facilities, or other public agencies or private nonprofit organizations providing services to victims of sexual assault or domestic violence. As used in this subdivision, "abuse against a child" means "child abuse" as defined in Section 11165.6 of the Penal Code and abuse against any of the other persons described in paragraph (2) or (3) means "abuse" as defined in Section 6203 ofthis code.

(c) The nature and amount of contact with both parents, except as provided in Section 3046.

(d) The habitual or continual illegal use of controlled substances or habitual or continual abuse of alcohol by either parent. Before considering these allegations, the court may first require independent corroboration, including, but not limited to, written reports from law enforcement agencies, courts, probation departments, social welfare agencies, medical facilities, rehabilitation facilities, or other public agencies or nonprofit organizations providing drug and alcohol abuse services. As used in this subdivision, "controlled substances" has the same meaning as defined in the California Uniform Controlled Substances Act, Division 10 (commencing with Section 11000) of the Health and Safety Code.

(e) (1) Where allegations about a parent pursuant to subdivision (b) or (d) have been brought to the attention of the court in the current proceeding, and the court makes an order for sole or joint custody to that parent, the court shall state its reasons in writing or on the record. In these circumstances, the court shall ensure that any order regarding custody or visitation is specific as to time, day, place, and manner of transfer of the child as set forth in subdivision (b) of Section 6323.

(2) The provisions of this subdivision shall not apply if the parties stipulate in writing or on the record regarding custody or visitation.

Family Code § 3042. (a) If a child is of sufficient age and capacity to reason so as to form an intelligent preference as to custody, the court shall consider and give due weight to the wishes of the child in making an order granting or modifying custody.

(b) In addition to the requirements of subdivision (b) of Section 765 of the Evidence Code, the court shall control the examination of the child witness so as to protect the best interests of the child. The court may preclude the calling of the child as a witness where the best interests of the child so dictate and may provide alternative means of obtaining information regarding the child's preferences.

Family Code § 3080. There is a presumption, affecting the burden of proof, that joint custody is in the best interest of a minor child, subject to Section 3011, where the parents have agreed to joint custody or so agree in open court at a hearing for the purpose of determining the custody of the minor child.

Family Code § 3085. In making an order for custody with respect to both parents, the court may grant joint legal custody without granting joint physical custody.

Family Code § 3086. In making an order of joint physical custody or joint legal custody, the court may specify one parent as the primary caretaker of the child and one home as the primary home of the child, for the purposes of determining eligibility for public assistance.

Family Code § 3087. An order for joint custody may be modified or terminated upon the petition of one or both parents or on the court's own motion if it is shown that the best interest of the child requires modification or termination of the order. If either parent opposes the modification or termination order, the court shall state in its decision the reasons for modification or termination of the joint custody order.

Exhibit B – Child Support

Family Code § 3585. The provisions of an agreement between the parents for child support shall be deemed to be separate and severable from all other provisions of the agreement relating to property and support of the wife or husband. An order for child support based on the agreement shall be law-imposed and shall be made under the power of the court to order child support

Family Code § 3586. If an agreement between the parents combines child support and spousal support without designating the amount to be paid for child support and the amount to be paid for spousal support, the court is not required to make a separate order for child support.

Family Code § 3587. Notwithstanding any other provision of law, the court has the authority to approve a stipulated agreement by the parents to pay for the support of an adult child or for the continuation of child support after a child attains the age of 18 years and to make a support order to effectuate the agreement.

Family Code § 4053. In implementing the statewide uniform guideline, the courts shall adhere to the following principles:

(a) A parent's first and principal obligation is to support his or her minor children according to the parent's circumstances and station in life.

(b) Both parents are mutually responsible for the support of their children.

(c) The guideline takes into account each parent's actual income and level of responsibility for the children.

(d) Each parent should pay for the support of the children according to his or her ability.

(e) The guideline seeks to place the interests of children as the state's top priority.

(f) Children should share in the standard of living of both parents. Child support may therefore appropriately improve the standard of living of the custodial household to improve the lives of the children.

(g) Child support orders in cases in which both parents have high levels of responsibility for the children should reflect the increased costs of raising the children in two homes and should minimize significant disparities in the children's living standards in the two homes.

(h) The financial needs of the children should be met through private financial resources as much as possible.

(i) It is presumed that a parent having primary physical responsibility for the children contributes a significant portion of available resources for the support of the children.

(j) The guideline seeks to encourage fair and efficient settlements of conflicts between parents and seeks to minimize the need for litigation.

(k) The guideline is intended to be presumptively correct in all cases, and only under special circumstances should child support orders fall below the child support mandated by the guideline formula.

(l) Child support orders must ensure that children actually receive fair, timely, and sufficient support reflecting the state's high standard of living and high costs of raising children compared to other states.

Family Code § 4055 (a) The statewide uniform guideline for determining child support orders is as follows:

$$CS = K (HN - (H\%) (TN)).$$

(b)   (1) The components of the formula are as follows:

(A) CS = child support amount.

(B) K = amount of both parents' income to be allocated for child support as set forth in paragraph (3).

(C) HN = high earner's net monthly disposable income.

(D) H% = approximate percentage of time that the high earner has or will have primary physical responsibility for the children compared to the other parent. In cases in which parents have different time-sharing arrangements for different children, H% equals the average of the approximate percentages of time the high earner parent spends with each child.

(E) TN = total net monthly disposable income of both parties.

(2) To compute net disposable income, see Section 4059.

(3) K (amount of both parents' income allocated for child support) equals one plus H% (if H% is less than or equal to 50 percent) or two minus H% (if H% is greater than 50 percent) times the following fraction:

Total Net Disposable Income Per Month	K
$0-800	0.20 + TN/16,000
$801-6,666	0.25
$6,667-10,000	0.10 + 1,000/TN
Over $10,000	0.12 + 800/TN

For example, if H% equals 20 percent and the total monthly net disposable income of the parents is $1,000, K = (1 + 0.20) X 0.25, or 0.30. If H% equals 80 percent and the total monthly net disposable income of the parents is $1,000, K = (2 - 0.80) X 0.25, or 0.30.

(4) For more than one child, multiply CS by:

2 children	1.6
3 children	2
4 children	2.3
5 children	2.5
6 children	2.625
7 children	2.75
8 children	2.813
9 children	2.844
10 children	2.86

(5) If the amount calculated under the formula results in a positive number, the higher earner shall pay that amount to the lower earner. If the amount calculated under the formula results in a negative number, the lower earner shall pay the absolute value of that amount to the higher earner.

(6) In any default proceeding where proof is by affidavit pursuant to Section 2336, or in any proceeding for child support in which a party fails to appear after being duly

noticed, H% shall be set at zero in the formula if the noncustodial parent is the higher earner or at 100 if the custodial parent is the higher earner, where there is no evidence presented demonstrating the percentage of time that the noncustodial parent has primary physical responsibility for the children. H% shall not be set as described above if the moving party in a default proceeding is the noncustodial parent or if the party who fails to appear after being duly noticed is the custodial parent. A statement by the party who is not in default as to the percentage of time that the noncustodial parent has primary physical responsibility for the children shall be deemed sufficient evidence.

(7) In all cases in which the net disposable income per month of the obligor is less than one thousand dollars ($1,000), the court shall rule on whether a low-income adjustment shall be made. The ruling shall be based on the facts presented to the court, the principles provided in Section 4053, and the impact of the contemplated adjustment on the respective net incomes of the obligor and the obligee. Where the court has ruled that a low-income adjustment shall be made, the child support amount otherwise determined under this section shall be reduced by an amount that is no greater than the amount calculated by multiplying the child support amount otherwise determined under this section by a fraction, the numerator of which is 1,000 minus the obligor's net disposable income per month, and the denominator of which is 1,000. If a low-income adjustment is allowed, the court shall state the reasons supporting the adjustment in writing or on the record and shall document the amount of the adjustment and the underlying facts and circumstances.

(8) Unless the court orders otherwise, the order for child support shall allocate the support amount so that the amount

of support for the youngest child is the amount of support for one child, and the amount for the next youngest child is the difference between that amount and the amount for two children, with similar allocations for additional children. However, this paragraph does not apply to cases in which there are different time-sharing arrangements for different children or where the court determines that the allocation would be inappropriate in the particular case.

(c) If a court uses a computer to calculate the child support order, the computer program shall not automatically default affirmatively or negatively on whether a low-income adjustment is to be applied. If the low-income adjustment is applied, the computer program shall not provide the amount of the low-income adjustment. Instead, the computer program shall ask the user whether or not to apply the low-income adjustment, and if answered affirmatively, the computer program shall provide the range of the adjustment permitted by paragraph (7) of subdivision (b).

Family Code § 4057 (a) The amount of child support established by the formula provided in subdivision (a) of Section 4055 is presumed to be the correct amount of child support to be ordered.

(b) The presumption of subdivision (a) is a rebuttable presumption affecting the burden of proof and may be rebutted by admissible evidence showing that application of the formula would be unjust or inappropriate in the particular case, consistent with the principles set forth in Section 4053, because one or more of the following factors is found to be applicable by a preponderance of the evidence, and the court states in writing or on the record the information required in subdivision (a) of Section 4056:

(1) The parties have stipulated to a different amount of child support under subdivision (a) of Section 4065.

(2) The sale of the family residence is deferred pursuant to Chapter 8 (commencing with Section 3800) of Part 1 and the rental value of the family residence in which the children reside exceeds the mortgage payments, homeowner's insurance, and property taxes. The amount of any adjustment pursuant to this paragraph shall not be greater than the excess amount.

(3) The parent being ordered to pay child support has an extraordinarily high income and the amount determined under the formula would exceed the needs of the children.

(4) A party is not contributing to the needs of the children at a level commensurate with that party's custodial time.

(5) Application of the formula would be unjust or inappropriate due to special circumstances in the particular case. These special circumstances include, but are not limited to, the following:

(A) Cases in which the parents have different time-sharing arrangements for different children.

(B) Cases in which both parents have substantially equal time-sharing of the children and one parent has a much lower or higher percentage of income used for housing than the other parent.

(C) Cases in which the children have special medical or other needs that could require child support that would be greater than the formula amount.

Family Code § 4057.5 (a)(1) The income of the obligor parent's subsequent spouse or nonmarital partner shall not be considered when determining or modifying child support, except in an extraordinary case where excluding that income would lead to extreme and severe hardship to any child subject to the child support award, in which case the court shall also consider whether including that income would lead to extreme and severe hardship to any child supported by the obligor or by the obligor's subsequent spouse or nonmarital partner.

(2) The income of the obligee parent's subsequent spouse or nonmarital partner shall not be considered when determining or modifying child support, except in an extraordinary case where excluding that income would lead to extreme and severe hardship to any child subject to the child support award, in which case the court shall also consider whether including that income would lead to extreme and severe hardship to any child supported by the obligee or by the obligee's subsequent spouse or nonmarital partner.

(b) For purposes of this section, an extraordinary case may include a parent who voluntarily or intentionally quits work or reduces income, or who intentionally remains unemployed or underemployed and relies on a subsequent spouse's income.

(c) If any portion of the income of either parent's subsequent spouse or nonmarital partner is allowed to be considered pursuant to this section, discovery for the purposes of determining income shall be based on W2 and 1099 income tax forms, except where the court determines that application would be unjust or inappropriate.

(d) If any portion of the income of either parent's subsequent spouse or nonmarital partner is allowed to be considered pursuant to this section, the court shall allow a hardship deduction based on the minimum living expenses for one or more stepchildren of the party subject to the order.

(e) The enactment of this section constitutes cause to bring an action for modification of a child support order entered prior to the operative date of this section.

Family Code § 4058 (a) The annual gross income of each parent means income from whatever source derived, except as specified in subdivision (c) and includes, but is not limited to, the following:

> (1) Income such as commissions, salaries, royalties, wages, bonuses, rents, dividends, pensions, interest, trust income, annuities, workers' compensation benefits, unemployment insurance benefits, disability insurance benefits, social security benefits, and spousal support actually received from a person not a party to the proceeding to establish a child support order under this article.

> (2) Income from the proprietorship of a business, such as gross receipts from the business reduced by expenditures required for the operation of the business.

> (3) In the discretion of the court, employee benefits or self-employment benefits, taking into consideration the benefit to the employee, any corresponding reduction in living expenses, and other relevant facts.

(b) The court may, in its discretion, consider the earning capacity of a parent in lieu of the parent's income, consistent with the best interests of the children.

(c) Annual gross income does not include any income derived from child support payments actually received, and income derived from any public assistance program, eligibility for which is based on a determination of need. Child support received by a party for children from another relationship shall not be included as part of that party's gross or net income.

Family Code § 4059. The annual net disposable income of each parent shall be computed by deducting from his or her annual gross income the actual amounts attributable to the following items or other items permitted under this article:

(a) The state and federal income tax liability resulting from the parties' taxable income. Federal and state income tax deductions shall bear an accurate relationship to the tax status of the parties (that is, single, married, married filing separately, or head of household) and number of dependents. State and federal income taxes shall be those actually payable (not necessarily current withholding) after considering appropriate filing status, all available exclusions, deductions, and credits. Unless the parties stipulate otherwise, the tax effects of spousal support shall not be considered in determining the net disposable income of the parties for determining child support, but shall be considered in determining spousal support consistent with Chapter 3 (commencing with Section 4330) of Part 3.

(b) Deductions attributed to the employee's contribution or the self-employed worker's contribution pursuant to the Federal Insurance Contributions Act (FICA), or an amount not to exceed that allowed under FICA for persons not subject to FICA, provided that the deducted amount is used to secure retirement or disability benefits for the parent.

(c) Deductions for mandatory union dues and retirement benefits, provided that they are required as a condition of employment.

(d) Deductions for health insurance or health plan premiums for the parent and for any children the parent has an obligation to support and deductions for state disability insurance premiums.

(e) Any child or spousal support actually being paid by the parent pursuant to a court order, to or for the benefit of any person who is not a subject of the order to be established by the court. In the absence of a court order, any child support actually being paid, not to exceed the amount established by the guideline, for natural or adopted children of the parent not residing in that parent's home, who are not the subject of the order to be established by the court, and of whom the parent has a duty of support. Unless the parent proves payment of the support, no deduction shall be allowed under this subdivision.

(f) Job-related expenses, if allowed by the court after consideration of whether the expenses are necessary, the benefit to the employee, and any other relevant facts.

(g) A deduction for hardship, as defined by Sections 4070 to 4073, inclusive, and applicable published appellate court decisions. The amount of the hardship shall not be deducted from the amount of child support, but shall be deducted from the income of the party to whom it applies. In applying any hardship under paragraph (2) of subdivision (a) of Section 4071, the court shall seek to provide equity between competing child support orders. The Judicial Council shall develop a formula for calculating the maximum hardship deduction and shall submit it to the Legislature for its consideration on or before July 1, 1995.

Family Code § 4060. The monthly net disposable income shall be computed by dividing the annual net disposable income by 12. If the monthly net disposable income figure does not accurately reflect the actual or prospective earnings of the parties at the time the determination of support is made, the court may adjust the amount appropriately.

Family Code § 4062 (a) The court shall order the following as additional child support:

(1) Childcare costs related to employment or to reasonably necessary education or training for employment skills.

(2) The reasonable uninsured health care costs for the children as provided in Section 4063.

(b) The court may order the following as additional child support:

(1) Costs related to the educational or other special needs of the children.

(2) Travel expenses for visitation.

Family Code § 4074. This article applies to an award for the support of children, including those awards designated as "family support," that contain provisions for the support of children as well as for the support of the spouse.

Exhibit C – Family Support

Family Code § 4066. Orders and stipulations otherwise in compliance with the statewide uniform guideline may designate as "family support" an unallocated total sum for support of the spouse and any children without specifically labeling all or any portion as "child support" as long as the amount is adjusted to reflect the effect of additional deductibility.

The amount of the order shall be adjusted to maximize the tax benefits for both parents.

Exhibit D – Spousal Support

Family Code § 4320. In ordering spousal support under this part, the court shall consider all of the following circumstances:

(a) The extent to which the earning capacity of each party is sufficient to maintain the standard of living established during the marriage, taking into account all of the following:

(1) The marketable skills of the supported party; the job market for those skills; the time and expenses required for the supported party to acquire the appropriate education or training to develop those skills; and the possible need for retraining or education to acquire other, more marketable skills or employment.

(2) The extent to which the supported party's present or future earning capacity is impaired by periods of unemployment that were incurred during the marriage to permit the supported party to devote time to domestic duties.

(b) The extent to which the supported party contributed to the attainment of an education, training, a career position, or a license by the supporting party.

(c) The ability to pay of the supporting party, taking into account the supporting party's earning capacity, earned and unearned income, assets, and standard of living.

(d) The needs of each party based on the standard of living established during the marriage.

(e) The obligations and assets, including the separate property, of each party.

(f) The duration of the marriage.

(g) The ability of the supported party to engage in gainful employment without unduly interfering with the interests of dependent children in the custody of the party.

(h) The age and health of the parties.

(i) The immediate and specific tax consequences to each party.

(j) The balance of the hardships to each party.

(k) The goal that the supported party shall be self-supporting within a reasonable period of time. A "reasonable period of time" for purposes of this section generally shall be one-half the length of the marriage. However, nothing in this section is intended to limit the court's discretion to order support for a greater or lesser length of time, based on any of the other factors listed in this section and the circumstances of the parties.

(l) Any other factors the court determines are just and equitable.

Family Code § 4323 (a) (1) Except as otherwise agreed to by the parties in writing, there is a rebuttable presumption, affecting the burden of proof, of decreased need for spousal support if the supported party is cohabiting with a person of the opposite sex. Upon a determination that circumstances have changed, the court may modify or terminate the spousal support as provided for in Chapter 6 (commencing with Section 3650) of Part 1. (2) Holding oneself out to be the husband or wife of the person with whom one is cohabiting is not necessary to constitute cohabitation as the term is used in this subdivision.

(b) The income of a supporting spouse's subsequent spouse or nonmarital partner shall not be considered when determining or modifying spousal support.

(c) Nothing in this section precludes later modification or termination of spousal support on proof of change of circumstances.

Exhibit E – Division of Property

Family Code § 2550. Except upon the written agreement of the parties, or on oral stipulation of the parties in open court, or as otherwise provided in this division, in a proceeding for dissolution of marriage or for legal separation of the parties, the court shall, either in its judgment of dissolution of the marriage, in its judgment of legal separation of the parties, or at a later time if it expressly reserves jurisdiction to make such a property division, divide the community estate of the parties equally.

Family Code § 2551. For the purposes of division and in confirming or assigning the liabilities of the parties for which the community estate is liable, the court shall characterize liabilities as separate or community and confirm or assign them to the parties in accordance with Part 6 (commencing with Section 2620).

Family Code § 2581. For the purpose of division of property on dissolution of marriage or legal separation of the parties, property acquired by the parties during marriage in joint form, including property held in tenancy in common, joint tenancy, or tenancy by the entirety, or as community property, is presumed to be community property. This presumption is a presumption affecting the burden of proof and may be rebutted by either of the following:

(a) A clear statement in the deed or other documentary evidence of title by which the property is acquired that the property is separate property and not community property.

(b) Proof that the parties have made a written agreement that the property is separate property.

Family Code § 2600. Notwithstanding Sections 2550 to 2552, inclusive, the court may divide the community estate as provided in this part.

Family Code § 2601. Where economic circumstances warrant, the court may award an asset of the community estate to one party on such conditions as the court deems proper to effect a substantially equal division of the community estate.

Family Code § 2602. As an additional award or offset against existing property, the court may award, from a party's share, the amount the court determines to have been deliberately misappropriated by the party to the exclusion of the interest of the other party in the community estate.

Family Code § 2603 (a) "Community estate personal injury damages" as used in this section means all money or other property received or to be received by a person in satisfaction of a judgment for damages for the person's personal injuries or pursuant to an agreement for the settlement or compromise of a claim for the damages, if the cause of action for the damages arose during the marriage but is not separate property as described in Section 781, unless the money or other property has been commingled with other assets of the community estate.

(b) Community estate personal injury damages shall be assigned to the party who suffered the injuries unless the court, after taking into account the economic condition and needs of each party, the time that has elapsed since the recovery of the damages or the accrual of the cause of action, and all other facts of the case, determines that the interests of justice require another disposition. In such a case, the community estate personal injury damages shall be assigned to the respective parties in such proportions as the court determines to be just, except that at least one-half of the damages shall be assigned to the party who suffered the injuries.

Family Code § 2610 (a) Except as provided in subdivision (b), the court shall make whatever orders are necessary or appropriate to ensure that each party receives the party's full community property share in any retirement plan, whether public or private, including all survivor and death benefits, including, but not limited to, any of the following:

(1) Order the disposition of any retirement benefits payable upon or after the death of either party in a manner consistent with Section 2550.

(2) Order a party to elect a survivor benefit annuity or other similar election for the benefit of the other party, as specified by the court, in any case in which a retirement plan provides for such an election, provided that no court shall order a retirement plan to provide increased benefits determined on the basis of actuarial value.

(3) Upon the agreement of the nonemployee spouse, order the division of accumulated community property contributions and service credit as provided in the following or similar enactments:

(A) Article 2 (commencing with Section 21290) of Chapter 9 of Part 3 of Division 5 of Title 2 of the Government Code.

(B) Chapter 12 (commencing with Section 22650) of Part 13 of the Education Code.

(C) Article 8.4 (commencing with Section 31685) of Chapter 3 of Part 3 of Division 4 of Title 3 of the Government Code.

(D) Article 2.5 (commencing with Section 75050) of Chapter 11 of Title 8 of the Government Code.

(E) Chapter 15 (commencing with Section 27400) of Part 14 of the Education Code.

(4) Order a retirement plan to make payments directly to a nonmember party of his or her community property interest in retirement benefits.

(b) A court shall not make any order that requires a retirement plan to do either of the following:

(1) Make payments in any manner that will result in an increase in the amount of benefits provided by the plan.

(2) Make the payment of benefits to any party at any time before the member retires, except as provided in paragraph (3) of subdivision (a), unless the plan so provides.

(c) This section shall not be applied retroactively to payments made by a retirement plan to any person who retired or died prior to January 1, 1987, or to payments made to any person who retired or died prior to June 1, 1988, for plans subject to paragraph (3) of subdivision (a).

Family Code § 2620. The debts for which the community estate is liable which are unpaid at the time of trial, or for which the community estate becomes liable after trial, shall be confirmed or divided as provided in this part.

Family Code § 2621. Debts incurred by either spouse before the date of marriage shall be confirmed without offset to the spouse who incurred the debt.

Family Code § 2622 (a) Except as provided in subdivision (b), debts incurred by either spouse after the date of marriage but before the date of separation shall be divided as set forth in Sections 2550 to 2552, inclusive, and Sections 2601 to 2604, inclusive.

(b) To the extent that community debts exceed total community and quasi-community assets, the excess of debt shall be assigned as the court deems just and equitable, taking into account factors such as the parties' relative ability to pay.

Family Code § 2623. Debts incurred by either spouse after the date of separation but before entry of a judgment of dissolution of marriage or legal separation of the parties shall be confirmed as follows:

(a) Debts incurred by either spouse for the common necessaries of life of either spouse or the necessaries of life of the children of the marriage for whom support may be ordered, in the absence of a court order or written agreement for support or for the payment of these debts, shall be confirmed to either spouse according to the parties' respective needs and abilities to pay at the time the debt was incurred.

(b) Debts incurred by either spouse for nonnecessaries of that spouse or children of the marriage for whom support may be ordered shall be confirmed without offset to the spouse who incurred the debt.

Family Code § 2624. Debts incurred by either spouse after entry of a judgment of dissolution of marriage but before termination of the parties' marital status or after entry of a judgment of legal separation of the parties shall be confirmed without offset to the spouse who incurred the debt.

Family Code § 2625. Notwithstanding Sections 2620 to 2624, inclusive, all separate debts, including those debts incurred by a spouse during marriage and before the date of separation that were not incurred for the benefit of the community, shall be confirmed without offset to the spouse who incurred the debt.

Family Code § 2626. The court has jurisdiction to order reimbursement in cases it deems appropriate for debts paid after separation but before trial.

Family Code § 2627. Notwithstanding Sections 2550 to 2552, inclusive, and Sections 2620 to 2624, inclusive, educational loans shall be assigned pursuant to Section 2641 and liabilities subject to paragraph (2) of subdivision (b) of Section 1000 shall be assigned to the spouse whose act or omission provided the basis for the liability, without offset.

Family Code § 2628. Notwithstanding Sections 2550 to 2552, inclusive, and Sections 2620 to 2624, inclusive, joint California income tax liabilities may be revised by a court in a proceeding for dissolution of marriage, provided the requirements of Section 19006 of the Revenue and Taxation Code are satisfied.

Family Code § 2640 (a) "Contributions to the acquisition of property," as used in this section, include downpayments, payments for improvements, and payments that reduce the principal of a loan used to finance the purchase or improvement of the property but do not include payments of interest on the loan or payments made for maintenance, insurance, or taxation of the property.

(b) In the division of the community estate under this division, unless a party has made a written waiver of the right to reimbursement or has signed a writing that has the effect of a waiver, the party shall be reimbursed for the party's contributions to the acquisition of property of the community property estate to the extent the party traces the contributions to a separate property source. The amount reimbursed shall be without interest or adjustment for change in monetary values and may not exceed the net value of the property at the time of the division.

(c) A party shall be reimbursed for the party's separate property contributions to the acquisition of property of the other spouse's separate property estate during the marriage, unless there has been a transmutation in writing pursuant to Chapter 5 (commencing with Section 850) of Part 2 of Division 4, or a written waiver of the right to reimbursement. The amount reimbursed shall be without interest or adjustment for change in monetary values and may not exceed the net value of the property at the time of the division.

Family Code § 2641 (a) "Community contributions to education or training" as used in this section means payments made with community or quasi-community property for education or training or for the repayment of a loan incurred for education or training, whether the payments were made while the parties were resident in this state or resident outside this state.

(b) Subject to the limitations provided in this section, upon dissolution of marriage or legal separation of the parties:

(1) The community shall be reimbursed for community contributions to education or training of a party that substantially enhances the earning capacity of the party. The amount reimbursed shall be with interest at the legal rate, accruing from the end of the calendar year in which the contributions were made.

(2) A loan incurred during marriage for the education or training of a party shall not be included among the liabilities of the community for the purpose of division pursuant to this division but shall be assigned for payment by the party.

(c) The reimbursement and assignment required by this section shall be reduced or modified to the extent circumstances render such a disposition unjust, including, but not limited to, any of the following:

(1) The community has substantially benefited from the education, training, or loan incurred for the education or training of the party. There is a rebuttable presumption, affecting the burden of proof, that the community has not substantially benefited from community contributions to the education or training made less than 10 years before the commencement of the proceeding, and that the community has substantially benefited from community contributions to the education or training made more than 10 years before the commencement of the proceeding.

(2) The education or training received by the party is offset by the education or training received by the other party for which community contributions have been made.

(3) The education or training enables the party receiving the education or training to engage in gainful employment that substantially reduces the need of the party for support that would otherwise be required.

(d) Reimbursement for community contributions and assignment of loans pursuant to this section is the exclusive remedy of the community or a party for the education or training and any resulting enhancement of the earning capacity of a party. However, nothing in this subdivision limits consideration of the effect of the education, training, or enhancement, or the amount reimbursed pursuant to this section, on the circumstances of the parties for the purpose of an order for support pursuant to Section 4320.

(e) This section is subject to an express written agreement of the parties to the contrary.

Family Code § 2650. In a proceeding for division of the community estate, the court has jurisdiction, at the request of either party, to divide the separate property interests of the parties in real and personal property, wherever situated and whenever acquired, held by the parties as joint tenants or tenants in common. The property shall be divided together with, and in accordance with the same procedure for and limitations on, division of the community estate.

Family Code § 2660 (a) Except as provided in subdivision (b), if the property subject to division includes real property situated in another state, the court shall, if possible, divide the community property and quasi-community property as provided for in this division in such a manner that it is not necessary to change the nature of the interests held in the real property situated in the other state.

(b) If it is not possible to divide the property in the manner provided for in subdivision (a), the court may do any of the following in order to effect a division of the property as provided for in this division:

(1) Require the parties to execute conveyances or take other actions with respect to the real property situated in the other state as are necessary.

(2) Award to the party who would have been benefited by the conveyances or other actions the money value of the interest in the property that the party would have received if the conveyances had been executed or other actions taken.

INDEX

A

Airline miles, 51
Alimony recapture, 96
Alimony, see *Spousal support*
Arbitration, 185
Assets
    appraisal of, 56-64
    division of, 45-82
    hiding of, 53-54
Audit, tax, 190

B

Bank account statements, 57
Bankruptcy, 76-77, 197
Bills, mediation, 188
Business, closely held, 58-59

C

Cash, 57
Childcare, 112
Child support, 101-114
    amount of, 103-105
    differing from statutory formula,
        109-111
    duration of, 108-109
    earning capacity and, 114
    new spouse income and, 111
    statutory formula regarding, 103
Collectibles, 57
Co-mediation, 18
Community property, 45, 78
Credit reports, 50
Custody, 143-180
    appointment of attorney for child
        and, 178
    arrangements, various, 147-153

Custody (cont.)
    childcare and, 172
    child's choice of parent and, 176-
        177
    decision making and, 162
    dispute resolution and, 163
    evaluators, 177
    ground rules and, 168
    holidays and, 161-162
    information exchange and, 166
    joint legal, 145
    joint physical, 145
    legal, 145
    moving and, 165, 178
    physical, 145
    primary physical, 145
    sole legal, 145
    sole physical, 145
    stepparents and, 173-176
    therapists and, 149

D

Debt, 70-75
    bankruptcy and, 76-77, 197
    division of, 70
    reimbursement of mortgage
        payments, 74
    use of community property to pay
        pre-marital debt, 71
    use of separate property to pay
        community property debt, 71
    use of separate property to pay
        community property debt after
        separation, 72-73
Defined benefit plans, 65
Defined contribution plans, 65
Discovery, expense of, 3

Divorce
  date of, 81
  expense of, 3-4
  forms required, see *Forms*
  process of, 39-44
  residency requirement, 39

E

Education of minors, 159-161
Employee Stock Ownership Plan
  (ESOP), 68
Epstein credits,140-141
Experts, expense of, 3

F

Family support, 97-99
Forms
  Declaration for Default or
    Uncontested Dissolution or
    Legal Separation, 41
  Declaration of Disclosure, 41
  Declaration of Residence, 41
  Declaration Regarding Service of
    Declaration Disclosure and
    Income and Expense
    Declaration, 44
  Declaration Under Uniform Child
    Custody Jurisdiction and
    Enforcement Act, 41
  Income and Expense Declaration,
    43
  Judgment, 44
  Notice of Entry of Judgment, 44
  Petition, 40
  Proof of Personal Service, 42
  Proof of Service by Mail, 42
  Schedule of Assets and Debts, 44
  Summons, 40
Frequent flyer points, see *Airline miles*

G

Gifts, 52

H

Health care expenses, 113,
  and parenting plan, 157-158

Home, 115-142
  calculating each spouse's share of,
    133
  calculating total monthly expenses
    relating to, 121-123
  capital gains tax and, 118
  capital gains tax exclusion related to
    sale of, 118-120
  comparative market analysis and,
    117
  cost of sale of, 124
  deferring the sale of, 130-132, 138
  estate planning and, 132
  fair market value of, 124
  installment loan and, 130
  living in prior to divorce, 139-140
  net equity value of, 124
  options regarding sale of, 116
  refinancing of, 130
  tax basis and, 120
  valuation of, 117-118

I

In re Marriage of Burgess, 179
In re Marriage of Carlson, 179
In re Marriage of Mardsen, 133, 135
In re Marriage of Moore, 133, 134
In re Marriage of Richmond, 94
Income, hiding of, 113-114
Individual Retirement Plan (IRA), 65
  Roth, 68
  traditional, 68
Insurance, life, 57
Insurance, health, 113

J

Joint tenancy, 132

L

Living trust, 183-184
    revocation of, 183
Loan applications, 51

M

Marital separation agreement, 44
Mediation, 6-37
    communication during, 19
    consulting an attorney during, 191
    listening during, 21
    stages of, 12-14
    when parties reside in different
        states, 195-196
Mediator
    attorney mediators, 16
    critical qualities of, 16
    experience of, 15
    part-time v. full-time, 17
    selecting a, 14
    therapist mediators, 16-17
    training of, 14
Memberships, clubs, etc., 52
Military pension, 60, 196

N

Net housing costs, 122
New partner/remarriage,
    child custody and, 173
    child support and, 111

P

Parenting plan, 145
    development of, 147
    residence of children and, 147-152
    ground rules and, 168
Pension, see *Defined benefit plans*
Power of Attorney, 184
Prenuptial agreements, 195
Privacy, mediation, 189, 192

Q

Qualified Domestic Relations Order
    (QDRO), 67-68
Quasi-community property, 80

R

Reimbursement
    of community property, 46, 71, 73
    of separate property, 46, 71-72
Residence, see *Home*
Restraining orders, mandatory, 42-43
Retirement plan
    division of, 65-69
    calculating value of, 68
    Social Security and, see *Social Security*
    taxation of, 68-69

S

Separate property, 45, 78
Separation, date of, 81
Social Security benefits, 195
Spousal support, 83-99
    amount of, 91-92
    duration of, 93-94
    effect of loss of employment on, 95
    indefinite, 84, 93
    marriages of long duration and, 83,
        95
    marriages of short duration and, 83,
        95
    modification of, 95
    recapture of, 96
    Richmond order and, 94
    taxes and, 96-97
    temporary, 91
Stock options, 60-64
    formulas for division of, 61, 62
    unvested, 60
    valuation of, 64
    vested, 60

T

Tax
    capital gains,
        upon sale of stock, 56
        upon sale of home, 118-120
    filing status, 193-194
    refunds, 51, 193
    returns, 48, 192
Tax Sheltered Annuities (TSAs), 68
Tentants in common, 132
Thrifts Savings Plan (TSP), 68
Timeshares, 52
Title reports, 50
Transmutation, 82
Travel expenses, 113
Tuition, 112-113

V

Vacation
    custody and, 150, 161-162
    pay, 51, 79

W

Watts claims, 140-141
Will and last testament, 182-183
    revocation of, 183, 185

Made in the USA
San Bernardino, CA
20 October 2015